YÜAN PORCELAIN AND STONEWARE

The Faber Monographs on Pottery and Porcelain

Former Editors: W. B. HONEY AND ARTHUR LANE
Present Editors: SIR HARRY GARNER and R. J. CHARLESTON

★

★

YÜAN PORCELAIN AND STONEWARE

by
MARGARET MEDLEY

FABER AND FABER
3 Queen Square
London

First published in 1974
by Faber and Faber Limited
3 Queen Square London WC1
Printed in Great Britain by
R. MacLehose and Company Limited
The University Press, Glasgow
All rights reserved

ISBN 0 571 10512 2

© *Margaret Medley, 1974*

FOREWORD

It is a paradox that the conquest of China by the Mongols in the thirteenth and fourteenth centuries introduced a freedom of artistic expression which enabled entirely new styles and techniques to be introduced in the decorative arts. Many of these came to full fruition in the early fifteenth century, but only during the last twenty years have scholars begun to see that the foundations for this golden age of the Ming dynasty were laid down a hundred years earlier.

In this, the first book to be devoted entirely to Yüan ceramics, Miss Medley has pursued with great thoroughness the main topic, the development of blue and white porcelain, destined to dominate not only Chinese porcelain in the future but also that of the whole world. But in addition she has dealt with the no less important porcellaneous wares and stonewares, such as the splendid southern celadons, the Tz'ŭ-chou wares and the southern brown stonewares, all of which brought many innovations. Her work has required exhaustive studies of the reports on recent excavations in China as well as of the early literature on the Yüan potteries. A critical examination of the techniques of potting has thrown new light on the remarkable ingenuity of the Chinese potters of the fourteenth century.

Yüan ceramics can no longer be relegated, as they have been in the past, to an inferior position among the Chinese decorative arts. There was tremendous experimentation, which produced failures at times. But in spite of their waywardness, the porcelains and stonewares of the Yüan dynasty have a freedom and vigour which will always give them a prominent place among the finest of Chinese ceramics.

HARRY M. GARNER

PREFACE

At the time when work on the following study was begun, the Yüan or Mongol period was still somewhat underrated or even ignored in the annals of art history. In the last few years, however, it has attracted attention and our view of this cataclysmic age has begun to undergo a transformation. In surveying the material brought together here I have had generous help from many friends and colleagues without whose assistance my task would have been immeasurably more difficult. I would like especially to express my gratitude to Sir Harry Garner, who invited me to take up the subject; his patient guidance on many points and his constant encouragement have been invaluable. Thanks are due to many museums in the United States, Japan, Europe and here in England for permission to illustrate their objects; I would also like to record my thanks to many collectors for permission to publish objects in their collections. They are too numerous to mention here in detail, but I have acknowledged them in the captions and in the text. To the staff of Sotheby's and Christie's, who have kindly helped with illustration, I am grateful for permission to draw on a number of unpublished and little known examples of the period which have passed through their sale rooms. I would particularly like to express my thanks to Mr. Henry Hodges of the Institute of Archaeology for his help and advice on technical points and for the drawings he supplied. In the matter of illustration I acknowledge a special debt to Mr. Paul Fox and Miss Vanessa Stamford of the Percival David Foundation for their willing cooperation in photographing material in the Collection to suit my particular needs and for undertaking a number of tedious processes on my behalf. Finally I acknowledge gratefully the work of Mr. G. Davenport and his staff of Birkbeck College in the preparation of the map.

March 1973   M.M.

CONTENTS

ILLUSTRATIONS

COLOUR PLATES

MONOCHROME PLATES
At the end of the book
(the references are approximate)

ILLUSTRATIONS

FIGURES IN THE TEXT

MAP

1

HISTORICAL AND STYLISTIC SETTING

In the history of Chinese ceramics, the Yüan period has been regarded in the past as an ugly duckling. If an object was of indifferent quality, or of no special aesthetic merit, there used to be a tendency to attribute it without further ado to the Yüan period. With specimens of high quality and exceptional aesthetic merit attribution was equally arbitrary and prompt to either the Sung dynasty, for celadon, Chün and Kuan wares for instance, or to the Ming for white wares, copper red and blue and white.[1] It has also been held that the Mongols had no real interest in the arts, that they did not find Chinese taste congenial, and that in consequence they neglected the creative arts. Within certain limits this judgement is true, and it has been assumed as the result that, ceramically speaking, the Yüan period was one of technical stagnation and aesthetic indigence. In the event nothing could be farther from the truth as the research of the last twenty years has proved. Although our knowledge of the period is still rudimentary on account of the exceptional difficulties with regard to textual and archaeological evidence in the broadest sense, a new picture of this brief hundred and fifty year period has begun to emerge. In terms of ceramic history the age of the Mongols is of fundamental importance to the development of the craft, technical advances being made without which the great attainments of the fifteenth century would have been impossible.

The Chinese artist-craftsman was always prepared to adopt new ideas, to digest, to transform and exploit them to suit the common taste, and it was perhaps the Mongols' greatest contribution that for the most part they remained aloof, neither apparently imposing standards, nor making exacting demands in terms of form or style. They thus indirectly left the potters, who had possibly become weary

[1] The problem is particularly acute as regards the northern wares and is discussed more fully in Chapter 5.

1

of the debilitating introspective tendencies and extreme refinement of Sung aristocratic taste, to explore new areas in both techniques and design. The only direct contribution to the ceramic industry made by the Mongols was the opening of intercourse with the west whereby new conceptions of form and decoration were enabled to penetrate.[1] The freedom from stringent control of the production was to bring its own reward, as was the new opportunity to respond to the stimulus of the foreign trade.

At the beginning of the twelfth century the Northern Sung dynasty was subjected to a humiliating defeat at the hands of the Jurchen Tartars from the north, who had first extinguished the Liao in Manchuria and the northernmost regions of China itself. In 1127 the Jurchen forced the Chinese court and government to flee south, thus bringing the Northern Sung to an abrupt and ignominious end, while they established themselves as the Chin dynasty in the territory north of a line from the Tsin-ling mountains in the west to the Huai river valley in the east. Less than a century later the Chin themselves were to be threatened by the Mongols, whose first step towards the domination of China was taken in 1208. In that year Genghis Khan, taking advantage of the death of the Chin ruler Chang-tsung, who was his suzerain, refused to recognize the new king, Wei-chao Wang, thus terminating his long-standing allegiance to the Chin people. Within three years of this event, the assault on north China began, and by 1215 Peking had fallen to the invaders. During the following eight years the pressure was maintained against the Chin, whose capital, now at K'ai-fêng on the Yellow river, was constantly threatened, not only from the north and west, but also from the eastern province of Shantung. The final destruction of the Chin and the total occupation of north China to as far south as the Huai river was accomplished by Genghis Khan's third son, Ogodaï, in 1234, surprisingly with the help of the Southern Sung, whose emperor committed the folly of seeking an alliance with the Mongols to help him in his own struggle against the Chin.[2] Thus was repeated the strategic error of the emperor Hui-tsung, who a century earlier had sought the help of the Chin against the Liao with such disastrous results. Ogodaï began his attack on the Southern Sung in the following

[1] For a recent study on this aspect see M. Medley, 'Chinese ceramics and Islamic design', *The Westward Spread of Chinese Influence*, Percival David Foundation Colloquies on the Art and Archaeology of Asia, No. 3, London, 1972, p. 1 ff.

[2] It is interesting to note that the Chinese were not the only people to fall to the Mongols as the result of such a trusting gesture. The Caliph in Baghdad also sought Mongol help against the Shahs of Khwarizm and ultimately suffered a similar fate. See B. Spuler, *The Mongol period* (*The Muslim World* Vol. II), Leiden, 1969, p. 8.

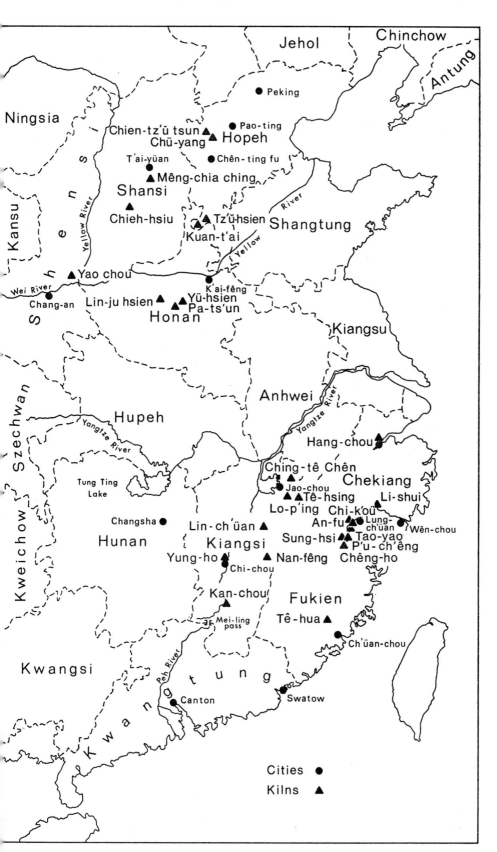

MAP SHOWING THE KILN SITES

year, but owing to squabbles among the Mongols themselves on the succession to the Great Khanate following the death of Ogodaï at the end of 1241, the threat of disaster was temporarily withdrawn. The final assault began in 1251, with pressure being exerted on the Chinese not from the north, but from the west, and the protracted campaign finally came to an end under Kublai Khan in 1275 following the fall of Hangchou.

For the first forty years of Mongol rule China existed in a state of relative peace. The vast territories of the new empire were systematically linked up by an efficiently policed network of roads, and trade passed freely into and out of China across Central Asia. With the renewed contact with western Asia came also the transmission in both directions of ideas and invigorating cultural influences. At the same time the sea-borne trade, along the south-east coast, much of it government sponsored and controlled, developed to a new level of prosperity with the help of the Arab and Persian communities at the ports down the coast from Ning-po in the north to Canton in the south. In Sung times the urgent need to maintain a strong defence against the northern tribes like the Khitans, the Hsi-hsia and the Jurchen had forced the Chinese government to exploit every possible means available to increase the revenue, and the means chosen that had the most far-reaching effects was that of taxing the foreign trade.[1] What in Sung times had been developed for reasons of economic expediency was further exploited by the Yüan rulers as part of a deliberate policy aimed at the extraction of the greatest possible wealth from the native Chinese for whom they cared nothing; they were in fact out for loot and luxurious living. It is particularly important to remember that although in Sung times there had grown up a new urban merchant class in a position to influence the trade to some extent, the real control of trade under the Yüan lay in the hands of the privileged foreigners, Persians, Arabs, Central Asians, Uighurs and many other alien peoples among whom we can number such a man as Marco Polo, whose allegiance was to the Mongol rulers rather than to the Chinese people. The Mongol practice of employing educated foreigners in the higher echelons of the administration in preference to the Chinese scholar-officials, whom they regarded with well-deserved suspicion, undoubtedly resulted in a fairly rapid influx of new ideas and techniques from abroad, of which some at least were quickly absorbed by the receptive Chinese. Some of these influences we recognize instantly in the art of the period. The most obvious one to spring to mind is, of course, the introduction of cobalt blue for the decoration of porcelain.

[1] Jitsuzō Kuwabara, P'u Shou-kêng, *Mémoires du Toyobunko*, Vol. 2, 1928, pp. 1–79 and Vol. 7, 1935, pp. 1–104.

HISTORICAL AND STYLISTIC SETTING

During the Sung period the port to carry the greatest volume of the overseas trade was Canton, but already during the Southern Sung a shift had begun to Ch'üan-chou in northern Fukien, about five hundred miles up the coast to the north. It was through this port, more conveniently placed in relation to the centres of the ceramic industry, that the enormous volume of trade flowed during the whole of the Yüan dynasty. It is significant that not only was there a large and flourishing Persian community resident in its own quarter in Ch'üan-chou, with its own mosques and cemeteries, but that at the end of the Sung and the beginning of the Yüan the Chief Superintendent of the Shipping was himself of Persian extraction and that his whole family, an extremely wealthy one, was engaged in the foreign trade, owning and operating a large fleet of ocean-going merchantmen.[1]

The increasing concentration of ceramic production in the south, particularly in the province of Kiangsi, with Chekiang and Fukien nearly as important in the industry, inevitably meant that the relatively convenient ports of Ch'üan-chou and later Wên-chou slightly farther north would be among those to which the merchants interested in the new products of the potteries would most frequently gravitate. Of all the provinces involved in the ceramic industry, Kiangsi and Chekiang were dominant, not so much on account of the number of kilns that were in operation as because of the phenomenal output and the increasing emphasis placed on high quality; later the Kiangsi kilns were to outstrip those of Chekiang on both counts. The numerous potteries of Jao-chou prefecture, which included those of Ching-tê Chên, were systematically developed during the Mongol period and became the main focus for both the domestic market and the foreign trade. The enormous output of this period and of the succeeding Ming is now sufficiently well known to require little further comment, but it is perhaps as well to bear in mind that the Chinese had no inhibitions whatever about the quality of the wares for export; almost everything could be and was sold. The wide variation in the quality of objects from excavations in South-east Asia, Indonesia and the Philippines, let alone the Islamic west, demonstrates this clearly; wasters and wares of so-called 'imperial' quality can be found in very close association in these areas, although generally speaking the trade to the Islamic west, especially to the eastern Mediterranean and to Persia seems to have been on a slightly higher level, the best being of superlative quality, and in greater quantity. The character of the wares for the Islamic market was in any case rather different from that intended for other Asian markets and there seems to have been a

[1] Ibid., Vol. 7, 1935, p. 39 and note 20, p. 57.

genuine willingness on the part of the Chinese to supply wares in forms agreeable to Muslim taste. The massive dishes, plates, jars and vases with their lavish decoration would appear to be evidence of this, and undoubtedly the increasing wealth of the Mamluke-dominated eastern seaboard of the Mediterranean and the Islamized Mongol Ilkhanate of Persia could well be expended on the best the Chinese were able to supply.[1] In fact it would seem that the greatest achievements in ceramics in the Yüan period were largely dependent for their initial inspiration upon the very lively interest shown by the foreign merchants in China's unique production. Imperial taste of the Mongol rulers in China did not direct the production of this era as it had done in the Sung and was to do again in the Ming, and we find export celadons and blue and white wares especially attaining standards in terms of quality and splendour of decoration that have rarely been surpassed except under strictly directed imperial patronage and in other periods.

The question of imperial patronage is a vexed one, which fortunately we can to a large extent ignore in studying the material of the late thirteenth and fourteenth centuries. Ceramic production was little affected by pretensions of imperial taste, in that each locality tended to continue the manufacture of the types of ware upon which it had been engaged in Sung times, though in many cases with a falling standard in terms of quality. This applied especially to the kilns in the north, such as those concentrating on the manufacture of Northern Celadon at centres like Yao-chou in Shensi, the Chün kilns of Lin-ju Hsien and Hao-pi-chi, though to a lesser extent in the main centres associated with the Tz'ŭ-chou type wares. Most of these northern centres suffered severely at the beginning of the twelfth century when the Khitans, and later the Jurchen Tartars, overran large areas. The Mongol invasion of the north at the beginning of the thirteenth century administered the *coup de grâce* to many of the kilns, only those in Honan and Hopei being able to survive the onslaught. The level of production in the kiln centres that succeeded in maintaining their identity often fell off, and in some cases, as at Yao-chou for instance, finally faded away, probably before the middle of the fourteenth century. A certain number of kilns in Hopei and Honan specializing in ordinary everyday white or black wares of rough strength continued to operate right through the fourteenth century, and a few continued into the Ming dynasty.

If the northern areas show some decline in both quality and quantity during the Yüan period, the reverse is true of the south. The establishment of the Sung court and government at Hangchou had

[1] See below, p. 34.

resulted effectually in shifting the economic focus of China to the southern provinces, a change which had begun some centuries earlier. The presence of a wealthy and demanding society not only stimulated those potteries already in operation to produce fine quality wares but also brought about the opening of many new kilns in Kiangsi, Chekiang, Fukien and Kuang-tung, where the resources of raw materials have subsequently proved almost inexhaustible. The variety of wares was as great as ever it had been in the north, and some types originally made in the north were to some degree imitated by the southern kilns. The most important advance in the ceramic field in the south was the concentration, not just on Jao-chou as a centre, but also on the white wares of the whole province. Thus the Yüan marks the beginning of the change-over from stonewares, that is wares fired at high temperatures with bodies varying in colour, to the fine white porcelains, hard, vitrified and translucent, that we now automatically associate with the name of China. There was at first the *ch'ing-pai*, and then other white wares of Jao-chou and those of Fukien, the latter which in later centuries were to achieve world-wide repute. These white wares were equalled in quality by the Chekiang celadons and some of the whitish bodied stonewares painted in black or brown on a pale creamy slip that were produced in the vicinity of Chi-chou in the southern end of the province of Kiangsi.

The great export trade in ceramics that had been fostered in the later years of the Southern Sung, was seized on and deliberately exploited by the Mongols, who were eager to squeeze the wealth out of their newly conquered empire. It was indeed their emphasis upon the monetary benefits of trade and industry, at the expense of agriculture, that was a major factor leading to their downfall. For their immediate purpose they were not slow to realize the immense profit to be reaped from the expansion of the export trade in ceramics, or indeed from the proper organization of the ceramic industry. On this last point we are surprisingly well informed since the local history of Fu-liang Hsien, compiled by Mongol orders in 1322, included a short work called *T'ao-ch'i lüeh*, usually translated 'Appendix to the Ceramic Records', by Chiang Ch'i, about whom nothing is known beyond the fact that he was apparently a man of some education who took the trouble to talk to the workmen engaged in the industry and learn some of the terminology, even if he did not always understand what was meant. The earliest surviving edition of this text dates from 1683 when it was included in a new, revised edition of the local history. It probably suffered some corruption in the course of the three hundred and fifty years between its composition and its inclusion in the K'ang-hsi edition of the *Fu-liang Hsien chih*, to give the local history its correct title. The information contained in the short and difficult text is of the greatest value in assessing the extent of the trade and the economic distribution of labour within the ceramic industry; it also has valuable information on certain aspects of technique. Among the source materials there is nothing comparable in the whole history of Chinese ceramics and it is unfortunate that the only available translation of it by Bushell is so full of errors as to be virtually useless.[1]

In Sung times, if we accept the implications of Chiang Ch'i's text, there was great leniency exercised in relation to the tax system for ceramics, with the consequence that the wealth and prosperity of the Fu-liang region was considerable. The Mongols no doubt appreciated this industrial prosperity and immediately set about the task of organizing it in such a way as to ensure that the bulk of the profits were siphoned off into their own coffers. During the Sung period, and possibly even earlier, it was the wares themselves and the commercial transactions in which they were involved as merchandise, that were subject to taxation, but with the establishment by the Mongols of a Fu-liang Porcelain Bureau between 1293 and 1295 'to control the kilns and the production of the porcelain',[2] the way was opened for the introduction of a new system of revenue collection. By the time Chiang Ch'i wrote his 'Appendix' this new system had clearly been in operation long enough to call forth no more than its bare description and the expression of the normal exasperated complaints against the rapacious and unjust habits of junior tax collectors, who extracted numerous unofficial fees over and above the accepted limits.

The system introduced was, briefly, that kilns had to be registered in accordance with a standard of measurement of capacity and the number of long-term craftsmen employed. The taxes were graded on the basis of this capacity and employment potential, and also on the basis of 'government approved sizes of vessels'; this last stipulation may have been carried over from the old Sung system. The kilns themselves could only be fired after the payment of a fee. The new regulations were evidently strict and offences against them might result not only in the imposition of a fine on the individual but might involve 'even the porters and merchants being collectively accused of the crimes'.[3] If an order came through from the capital for the supply of wares for the central government, a time limit was set for the completion of the order, which if not adhered to resulted in a great deal of unwelcome chivying of the craftsmen and additional

---

[1] S. Bushell, *Oriental Ceramic Art*, pp. 177–83.
[2] *Yüan Shih*, Ch. 88, f. 6a (*Ssŭ-pa pei-yao* edn.).
[3] *Fu-liang Hsien Chih*, Ch. 4, f. 47a, 1683 edn.

financial exactions. In spite of the regulations, restrictions, unofficial exactions by the authorities and the large dues payable to the county and provincial government, the ceramic industry contrived to remain a thriving one. The market supplied was very large, and according to Chiang Ch'i there was a ready sale even for wasters. The preferences of the different provinces were considered and carefully catered for to the material advantage of the potteries. It is worth noticing that the Fu-liang area was not the only one with a large and thriving ceramic industry in south China at this time. Chiang names a number of areas where there was a large production, among which were Chien-yang in Fukien, Nan-fêng in Kiangsi and Lung-ch'üan in Chekiang and he adds to this list Chên-ting in the north, in the province of Hopei, which he says produced 'red wares'. The descriptions he gives of the products do not, as a general rule, justify positive identification with the wares with which we are familiar today, but hints are to be found in his text which seem to support our attributions to the fourteenth century of at least some of the types we know.

In view of what has been explained up to this point it is clear that the study of Chinese ceramics under the Mongols involves the acceptance of certain previously neglected facts. In the first place we have to remember that China came under alien control in 1127, and under specifically Mongol domination about a century later, approximately half a century before the final collapse of the Southern Sung dynasty. We also have to recognize that the date 1280 for the establishment of the Yüan dynasty is a conventional one and somewhat unrealistic. The Mongols were in effective control of most of China including the important province of Kiangsi by 1273, and there remained after this date only isolated pockets of resistance along the south and south-east coasts. We are thus faced with the need when discussing ceramics particularly of the twelfth and thirteenth centuries to specify not the dynastic attribution of the piece we are discussing, but the approximate century or part of century, and if possible to make clear the centre or area in which it was produced.

When we turn our attention to the wares themselves the chronology of the Mongol conquest becomes important in as much as the stylistic elements found in the north differ noticeably from those current in the south until some time after the new rulers had established themselves securely in what had been the Southern Sung empire. A boldness and spontaneity of treatment, often highly individual and characteristic of a specific locality, was already common in the north even under the Chin rulers in the wares of Tz'ŭ-chou type (Plate 93). Certain elements in the decoration of this ware particularly are distinctively northern in origin; for instance the angular meander seen just below the main field of the jar illustrated on Plate 96A: this appears in the decorative repertoire of north China at least three centuries before we find it in the south in such wares as the blue and white and the dark brown painted wares from the Yung-ho kilns near Chi-chou (Plate 114), which do not appear to date before the beginning of the fourteenth century.[1] The ogival panel, with double or triple outline, is another motif the transmission of which is found to be from north to south, though the introduction of this motif at Ching-tê Chên may have been direct from Islam with the appearance of cobalt blue.[2] On the other hand the moniliform border or beading line seen on the jar in Colour Plate B, is a uniquely southern element of decoration, which is first found on the Buddhist Bodhisattva figures of *ch'ing-pai* type, as part of the jewelled ornamentation and taken over later as a relief decoration on vases, jars, cups and plates (Plates 7–13), and which does not appear at all on any of the wares that can be attributed to the northern kilns.

The dating of Yüan ceramics presents unusual difficulties with regard to some of the northern wares, mainly on account of the long persistence of certain decorative elements such as the two already mentioned. This combined with the naturally conservative attitude of the potters in this area towards changes in form, makes it particularly hazardous to attempt attributions within narrow limits. For such wares as Chün and the Northern Celadon there are also problems in connection with local style, but some of these have at least been partially resolved by recent archaeological work carried out by the Chinese, numerous reports of which have been published in the last dozen or so years. The southern wares, of which there is a great variety, are in some respects easier to deal with, especially in the fourteenth century. The large body of material available, especially of blue and white and celadon, makes the possibility of closer dating than hitherto a practical one, the more so as a few dated pieces give us a number of *points d'appui*. It is also fortunate that in the fourteenth century the expanding market, combined with a more adventurous spirit than that revealed in the north, brought about comparatively rapid changes in forms and styles, together with changes in technique.

The evolution of form and style in the Yüan period is of exceptional interest, serving as it does to reflect the liveliness in character of the craft and the adaptability of the industry under organized commercial direction. Like the sleeper awakening, the Chinese potter seems to be

[1] M. Medley, *Metalwork and Chinese ceramics*, Percival David Foundation Monograph Series, No. 2, 1972, p. 17 ff.

[2] M. Medley, *Chinese ceramics and Islamic design*, p. 3.

stretching himself, reaching out to exploit anew the potentiality of his material, expressing himself with spontaneity and a strength which had perhaps begun to fail a little in the Southern Sung period. While much of the elegance and refinement of form and the restrained treatment of surface was abandoned, perhaps to a collector's eye regrettably, there was a compensating factor to be found in the robust, vigorously handled forms and a flexibility in the approach to decoration in both technique and style. A period of frank experiment, breaking completely with the traditional Sung canon of taste, is followed shortly before the middle of the fourteenth century by the acceptance of only some of the techniques and styles in which the craftsmen had been trying out effects. What was accepted was refined until the elements became stabilized into what Pope has referred to as 'fourteenth century style'.[1] This is revealed in the painted wares with their splendour and complexity, in the apparently arbitrary placing of contrasting motifs, and with what seems superficially to be a total disregard of the natural contours of the vessel.[2] We see this well in such massive pieces as the wine jars on Colour Plates B and D and Plates 45A and 45B, and in the *mei-p'ing* vases (Plates 40 and 42A and B).

One of the most puzzling features of Chinese art that from time to time comes to the surface, is the tendency not only to divide the surface up into a series of horizontal bands without regard for contour, but also to combine a series of wholly unrelated and indeed often rhythmically opposed elements in such a way that the visual harmony is not disrupted. There are of course exceptions such as may be seen on a number of rather small pieces, most of them dating from what has been regarded as an early stage in the development of blue and white (Plates 22 and 39B). The main reason why this almost capricious treatment does not strike a jarring note, except in such a case as for instance the Tz'ŭ-chou piece on Plate 97, seems to be the extraordinary sensitivity of the Chinese artistic mind to the nice adjustment of proportions of the parts in relation not only to each other, but also to the whole on a particular surface and in a particular medium. A secondary reason is probably the unfaltering control of line, in both form and decoration; it has a fluency and elasticity that is immediately either exciting or soothing and which has a rhythm and vitality that binds the designs together with an irresistible dynamic strength. The assurance with which the Chinese potter approaches problems of form and design is what really singles him out as being among the greatest of creative artists. In the Yüan period he achieves in his own

[1] J. Pope, *Fourteenth Century Blue and White*, p. 50.
[2] M. Medley, op. cit., p. 4.

medium a power in the handling of form and in the enrichment of surface, such as the T'ang silverworker alone had achieved before him. The influence, both direct and indirect, of the Yüan potter has never been fully understood or appreciated, but we can be in no doubt as to the magnificence and integrity of his achievements, open-minded as he was to all the possibilities and self-assured in his handling of the material.

2

THE WHITE WARES OF JAO-CHOU

It is not possible fully to appreciate the aesthetic and technical revolution that took place in the white wares in the course of the Yüan dynasty without recalling the traditions of the Sung dynasty, with their emphasis on restraint in form and decoration, and the refinement of finish that appears endemic to the whole of Sung production. The changes that occurred in the late thirteenth and early fourteenth centuries are more strikingly seen in the porcelain of Jao-chou in the province of Kiangsi than in any of the wares from Chi-chou farther south, or from Tê-hua in Fukien, where the kilns were farther removed from the main centre of patronage in Hang-chou. After the transfer of the Sung capital from K'ai-fêng in the north to Hang-chou in northern Chekiang in 1128, there was inevitably an increase in the patronage of the southern kilns, and with them especially those of the Jao-chou area, which had long been producing high quality ceramics.[1] As a natural consequence of this change certain northern characteristics are to be found in the products of this important area, and the potters of Jao-chou at first drew heavily on the repertory of forms and decorations as well as on techniques which had at first been developed in the north, particularly at the Ting group of kilns.

During Sung times there was a unity of form, and a unity of decoration; the techniques, too, seem to have been fairly uniform among the white wares, carving, incising and moulding being common to the north, moulding having been introduced only after the other techniques had been thoroughly mastered. These techniques gradually filtered through to the south, moulding, as in the north, coming rather later into the range of decorative techniques employed. The carved decorations of *ch'ing-pai*, associated with the south, give an immediate impression of an artistic climate held in common with Ting and certain groups of Northern Celadon, which reflects the refinement of taste associated almost axiomatically with

[1] See above, Chapter 1, p. 5.

13

the restrained, and often introspective attitude of the age. Jao-chou, as the focal area of the south for the production of *ch'ing-pai*, shows this very clearly in so far as it is possible to trace wares back to this region. Assumptions must necessarily be made here, since archaeological evidence is not readily accessible. At the present time it is reasonable to accept the tradition that Jao-chou, which had first come into production in the T'ang dynasty, though somewhat intermittently,[1] began to develop a clearly defined range of white porcelains during the Sung, the potters, however, seeming only to have worked at times when the demands of agriculture were not too exacting, or when the season was bad. Chiang Ch'i in *T'ao-ch'i lüeh*, quoting an earlier text now lost, infers that the local population turned to pottery making in the bad seasons in order to maintain a bearable standard of living. It would be natural under this kind of economic pressure for an area so rich in the resources essential to the craft to develop rapidly during the twelfth century, when the centre of patronage moved south and brought the region within the field of its influence. The value of this stimulus combined with the wealth of experience among the potters and the easily accessible materials can hardly be doubted.

Although Jao-chou was a well-established centre of production, it seems only to have been in about the beginning of the thirteenth century, if we accept Chiang Ch'i's comments, that a deliberate policy of industrialization was initiated. In this it would seem that the merchants, gathered together in syndicates, provided the necessary capital to finance a high level of production, arranged transport and the distribution of the output over a large area, and handled the sales for the export trade, which at this time was being encouraged by the government for economic reasons.

The Sung taste for elegant simple forms and fluent well-balanced floral decorations carved into the body before glazing persisted for a time in the Yüan period, as did the liking for a seemingly frail translucent body carefully turned. It was surprising that the pieces retained their shape through the firing. During the Yüan period this frail elegance gave way to a heavier type of construction, and a more robust treatment was preferred in every respect. The main types of ware produced during the period were the *ch'ing-pai* and the so-called Shu-fu, with mid-way between the two a somewhat variable group of porcelains, which are best described as transitional white wares. These last and the Shu-fu both stem from the more deeply rooted *ch'ing-pai*, and the relationships between all three are close, with some developments running parallel. It is necessary to bear in

---

[1] Chiang Ch'i, *T'ao-ch'i lüeh* ('Appendix to the Ceramic Records'), *Fu-liang Hsien chih* ('History of Fu-liang Hsien') K'ang-hsi, 1683 edn.

mind that a large number of kilns were in operation in the late thirteenth century, and that because archaeological evidence on specific kilns is extremely meagre, it is only possible to refer to types in broad terms. Among the kilns known to have produced *ch'ing-pai*, however, are Hu-t'ien, Nan-shan and Hsiang-hu; the two former also produced blue and white.[1] There were probably many more kilns involved, and the transitional white wares may have come from any one of these. It is also of particular importance to notice that with only one exception so far, tomb finds of *ch'ing-pai* are confined to the more southerly regions of China, and with that one exception none north of Anhui, the bulk of the finds being from Kiangsi itself, Chekiang, Hupei and Hunan. Apart from these finds the most considerable body of material of this type has been found in south-east Asia, Indonesia, Fostat in Egypt, and quite recently from new archaeological sites of great interest and importance in the Philippines. The porcelains of this type that we now attribute to the Yüan period are often larger, nearly always slightly heavier, thicker near the base, with the foot-ring more roughly cut, and with a glaze often more blue in tone than is usual on the finer pieces of the earlier periods. The incised decoration, while stylistically imitating that of the northern ware, shows a tendency towards heaviness of outline, and the use of heavier and more emphatic combing than is found on the earlier Ting wares of the Northern Sung period and the period of the Chin dynasty in the eleventh and twelfth centuries. In addition the glaze, which as already pointed out may be more blue in tone, seems often to be rather thin near the rim of the bowls and displays imperfections of surface, usually as pitting and ferruginous staining, that are rare in those pieces generally assigned to the Sung dynasty. It was probably towards the end of the twelfth and during the early years of the thirteenth century that the practice in the south of firing bowls upside down on the rim was introduced, in imitation of Ting with its unglazed rim. Although the technique, often with rather a wide unglazed band at the rim, continued well into the fourteenth century on some types of *ch'ing-pai*, it was gradually abandoned as new styles and forms began to appear and gain popularity. Many of the pieces with the wide unglazed area at the rim seem to have been bound with silver, and occasionally one encounters examples on which fragments of such a band still survive. An additional reason for giving up the practice of firing bowls on the rim may have been that it was discovered that the rather non-plastic body of true poreclain was less

---

[1] A. D. Brankston, 'An excursion to Ching-tê-chên and Chi-an-fu in Kiangsi', *Transactions of the Oriental Ceramic Society*, 16, 1938–39, pp. 19–32; see especially pp. 22–3.

liable to warping and collapse at high temperatures than the semi-porcelain of Ting type. Another process that became common early in the thirteenth century was moulding, again an introduction from the north, and one of fundamental importance to the industrial development of the southern kilns, since the technique opened the way for a complex series of mass-production methods, that were to enable the kilns to maintain a steady output in the face of increasingly urgent demands for porcelain both at home and overseas.

In order to comprehend the course of the evolution of these porcelains it is essential to define the types that are involved in the following discussion. First there is *ch'ing-pai*, a characteristic white porcelain generally associated with the Sung period, but which we now know continued well into the fourteenth century. The body, very white and fine grained, with a glassy fracture, is covered with a transparent glaze faintly tinged with blue or green. The glaze is applied over a plain surface, or an incised and carved decoration, or over a moulded design. The foot-ring is usually thin and low, and if the piece has been fired on the rim, the glaze covers the foot-ring. The type is easily distinguished also by the thinness of the body and by the high gloss of the glaze. The second porcelain is that to which the name Shu-fu has been attached; the name is usually interpreted 'Privy Council' and is associated with the ware believed to have been made for the imperial Yüan household.[1] It is very much thicker and heavier in body than *ch'ing-pai*, and much more consistent in the form of the foot-ring, which is thicker and square cut; the decoration is always moulded on the inside, but sometimes with incised ornament on the outside, and the glaze is thick and often opaque and matt, being tinged with faint blue or grey. Between these two easily distinguished extremes, the *ch'ing-pai*, thin, light in weight and clear in glaze, and the Shu-fu, thick, heavy and often opaque in glaze, is a considerable group of porcelains, which for convenience may be termed transitional white wares. This large body of material is variable in the quality of both body and glaze, in weight in relation to size and shape, and in the cutting of the foot-ring. Some pieces are nearer to *ch'ing-pai* and others incline towards Shu-fu, sometimes one characteristic being dominant and sometimes another. In spite of the difficulties presented by this third group the main lines along which the white wares developed in the late thirteenth century and early fourteenth century towards a distinctive Yüan style can be described, but only in rather general terms owing to the lack of precisely dated material. One point that emerges from the study of such material as is available, is that the sensitive handling of form

[1] Ts'ao Chao in *Ko-ku yao-lun*, Ch. 3, is the first to give the name.

16

and the rather delicate treatment of surface, as represented by the bowl with lightly dotted combing such as those discussed and illustrated by Wirgin,[1] soon proved to be unacceptable to the changing taste of the late thirteenth century. The heavier, more robust forms, already mentioned, began quite rapidly to replace the refined types of the Sung tradition, partly perhaps as the result of the widening market both at home and abroad. What was lost in refinement and perfection of finish, however, was more than equalled by the new strength and ebullience of form, and the spontaneity of the decoration.

In bowls, saucers and small boxes many of the old habits both in technique and decoration were retained, the pieces in many cases continuing the traditional patterns, but often the quality of the craftsmanship declined under the pressure of demand. The increasing demands may have been an important factor in forcing the change towards stronger and heavier pieces in which the slow, highly skilled process of turning was reduced to a minimum. The demand for greater quantities undoubtedly put pressure on the potters to develop techniques which would simplify production and make it possible to meet demands by using relatively unskilled labour, and it is likely to have been this need that accounted for the increasing use of moulds. Mould-made bowls, fired on the rim, and small boxes similarly constructed, show a marked increase in numbers towards the end of the thirteenth century, most of them using designs that at first derive from the northern tradition, with decorations at least on the bowls that continue the type of decoration in which birds and flowers are disposed so as to encircle and revolve around a central motif, while at the rim is a key-fret border (Plate 1B). In these is found another feature indicative of a changing approach, for the designs while retaining the basic themes of Ting in the north, are more heavily treated, and at the same time the key-fret loses its precision, often being executed in a sketchy manner that suggests a misinterpretation of the motif, or, more likely an unconscious groping towards a new theme. It was not long before other decorations began to appear that were at variance with previously accepted conceptions of good design. The revolving decoration (Plates 1A, B) on bowls was gradually replaced by a compartmented scheme, or by a scheme built up on a series of concentric zones. The new approach broke down the old continuous rhythm and replaced it with a series of panels, usually six, each having its own decoration, sometimes only remotely related to that in the adjacent panel, and the whole only making a coherent scheme on the basis of the proportion of the parts to each other and to the whole. An example of this unusual approach to design in *ch'ing-pai* is seen in a bowl in the

[1] J. Wirgin, *Sung Ceramic Designs*, p. 48 ff., Plates 13a, b.

Ashmolean Museum (Plate 2B). This type has usually been pressed out very thinly, and occasionally added force is given to the panelling by notching the rim to suggest lobes; such an artificial device is probably no more than the survival of an old convention. In ways such as these the transition is made from an old style to a new and in some respects more lively one.

The technique of moulding was not confined to bowls and saucers, but was also particularly common in the manufacture of boxes and small jars. Boxes, either of simple cylindrical or multi-lobed cylindrical form (Plate 2A) dependent upon silver prototypes could be pressed out rapidly and accurately in large numbers without the need for any remarkable skill.[1] The decorations on the tops of these boxes are very varied, and there are many close parallels with metal-work, such as those found among the excavated material at Tê-yang in Ssŭ-ch'üan, which illustrates clearly the intimate relationship between the ceramics of the Yüan period and the metalworking traditions of the immediately preceding decades.[2] The repoussé and embossing techniques in silverwork lend themselves particularly well to imitation using moulding techniques in ceramic materials, and the Yüan potters, never averse to experiment, undoubtedly took advantage of the technical inspiration implicit in the decoration of other media available. They extended this moulding technique, often with elaborate decoration to small jars of which large numbers are known, especially from excavations at Santa Ana and Laguna la Bay in the Philippines, though some of this material may date well on into the fourteenth century.[3]

Carving and incising decoration on bowls, vases and other vessels also continue into the new era of Yüan, but like moulding, the style undergoes a transformation. In the Sung period a delicate, subtly controlled style, favouring floral motifs, had been preferred, and the use of combing, and what has been called 'dotted combing'[4] had been restrained towards the end of the thirteenth century, but now floral decorations, though still popular, are joined by dragon designs, and designs with small children, sometimes among flowers and intricate scrolling motifs (Plate 1A). The introduction of children in ceramic decoration is nearly always an indication of a mature stage, occurring late in the development of a ware, though it is possible in this

[1] The Nelson Gallery engraved and embossed silver box shown in the Cleveland Exhibition 'Chinese Art under the Mongols', 1968, No. 33f, is an excellent example of the type from which the ceramic ones are derived.
[2] *Wên-wu*, 1961, No. 11, pp. 48–55. In Chinese.
[3] See below, pp. 29–30.
[4] A term introduced by Dr. Bo Gyllensvärd in *Chinese Ceramics in the Carl Kempe Collection*, p. 20.

instance that the motifs were transmitted from the north where they had already been in use for some time in Northern Celadon and in the Tz'ŭ-chou types.[1] In addition the restrained use of the comb is abandoned in favour of a bolder and heavier use of this and similar tools, so that backgrounds frequently appear somewhat emphatically hatched. Bowls, plates and small saucers continue to be popular forms, and on these the new tendencies in style and technique are perhaps less striking than on the vases (Colour Plate A).

The bottle vases and other similar vertical forms are those that make one most keenly aware of the changes taking place, the strongest impact being made by the ever popular *mei-p'ing*. Not only does the decoration undergo the kind of transformation described, but even the forms themselves change. The carefully controlled elegance and subtle curvature of the Sung contour is replaced about the turn of the thirteenth and fourteenth century by a careless spontaneity and a more determined curvature. Bottle vases acquire narrower necks (Plate 3) and wider bases, while the *mei-p'ing* gain higher shoulders and a more emphatic turn downwards, giving them a more chunky appearance (Plates 4, 5); they, too, are wider at the base than formerly so that the elegant tapering of, for instance, the Tz'ŭ-chou type of the Sung period is eliminated from the repertory (Plate 5). This may be felt to be a loss, but the decoration, on account of its boldness, combines well with the change in form and is impressive in its refreshing freedom from restraint, a feature that imparts a new vitality to what one might consider a debilitated tradition.

In the treatment of the decorations themselves in these and other vases and jars there are two approaches. Either the decorations romp freely over the whole surface with an exuberant flamboyance, as in the case of the surprisingly blue toned *mei-p'ing* in the Victoria and Albert Museum (Colour Plate A), or it is confined to carefully defined bands, as in the case of the Boston *mei-p'ing* (Plate 5) or the Toronto vase (Plate 3). Here, as with the saucers and bowls with moulded decoration, there is once more in evidence the juxtaposing of un-related elements in a series of bands on the one surface. Of the two treatments the first, with the all-over scheme, is the earlier in date, for it carries on elements of the Sung style that were formerly best expressed in the Tz'ŭ-chou type stonewares. The second style probably begins in the recognizably Yüan form around the turn of the century, that is at about the same time as the forms begin to change; to attempt closer dating in the absence of archaeological evidence would not be justifiable. In the technique of carving the decoration, the older traditions are of course still continuing at this

[1] See below pp. 90 and 120.

stage. Nevertheless in the white wares there is a connection with another technique, also ultimately of northern origin. This is the use of slip, which in Tz'ŭ-chou wares had been incised or cut away to the body. In the white wares the slip is used rather differently and with much greater restraint; it is raised in relief and is often carefully combined with the normal use of carving and incising. Only on rare occasions is slip relief decoration used alone (Plates 6A, B), the more usual practice being to combine it with carving especially when the design is worked out in a series of horizontally organized bands.

At this point it becomes virtually impossible to confine oneself to the real *ch'ing-pai*, for the kilns were beginning to develop new bodies and glazes. Some bodies were very light in weight and others rather heavy; similarly some glazes were perfectly translucent, whether applied thinly or thickly, and others varied in opacity as well as in thickness. So much is this the case that no good purpose can be served by attempting to lay down any rules. The most that can be said is that the transitional white wares, which have a slightly more opaque glaze than is usually found in the true *ch'ing-pai*, are somewhat more variable in the character of the body, and the type seems to have begun around 1300. The decorative technique of carving and incising was common to both *ch'ing-pai* and transitional white wares, but the addition of slip relief decoration only occurs on the transitional whites, the technique of moulding being a later introduction to the transitional types, as was also the use of applied reliefs of the kind seen on the Ashmolean vase and on that from Cincinnati with slip reliefs (Plates 6A, B).

The organization of the decoration on the surface of vases, jars and bottles, which is now so frequently at variance with the older tradition of a free handling over the surface, initiates the style of the fourteenth century that was to attain maturity in the blue and white. The bands of decoration are broadly three in number, two of them being formal in character. These two formal bands constitute notional borders, one above and one below a naturalistically handled central band, framing it and giving it emphasis. The lower border is almost invariably of petal panels, and the upper one of triangular motifs or stiff leaves rising up the neck of a bottle; but on the shoulder of a jar or *mei-p'ing* (Plate 5) a more or less formalized lotus scroll winds round to replace the limiting angular motif. The central band, generally freely and vigorously cut is often of a three-clawed dragon on a tersely hatched ground, a pair of phoenixes or a lotus scroll. The base is usually quite roughly finished, the glaze only partly covering it, and a small amount of grit may adhere to the carelessly knife-trimmed foot-ring. A feature of the bottle vases, which suggests that they were all pro-

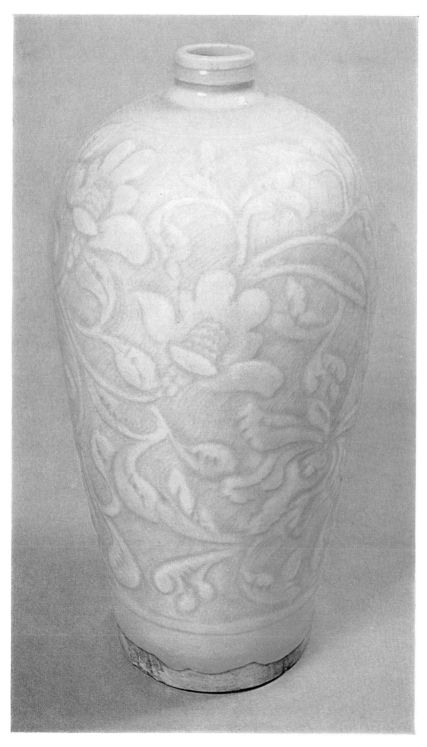

A. Mei-p'ing *vase*. Ch'ing-pai *ware. Ht.* 23·9 *cm.*
Victoria and Albert Museum

duced at one kiln, and perhaps over a relatively short period, is the weight in relation to size. They are nearly all exceptionally light in weight, while the *mei-p'ing* and the jars are much heavier, yet both in some instances carry the same decoration. The Boston *mei-p'ing* (Plate 5) and the Toronto bottle vase (Plate 3) demonstrate this point exceptionally clearly. This group, and its close relatives, would seem to date from the first two decades of the fourteenth century and may have begun shortly before the turn of the century. They constitute the main link between the final stages of the Sung style and the first fully developed stage of the Yüan style in the fourteenth century. There are examples, certainly not many, in which additional techniques—somewhat strange in the context—are employed.

The first supplementary technique is the use of beaded relief elements (Plates 7A, B), and the second is that of cutting away panels on the surface of the body and then filling them with moulded reliefs plugged into place with small lumps of clay. The classic example of this is the Fonthill vase now in the National Museum of Ireland in Dublin (Plate 7A), which Arthur Lane dated to the first quarter of the fourteenth century.[1] This vase is of very great importance in the history of ceramics as a whole and especially in the history of collecting in Europe, because it is the earliest piece of Chinese porcelain to be recorded in Europe. It was so obviously valued that it was not only provided with silver gilt and enamelled mounts, now missing, which transformed it into a ewer, but was esteemed worthy for presentation in or soon after 1381 to Charles III of Durazzo by Louis the Great of Hungary following the former's successful invasion and possession of the Kingdom of Naples subsequently to be crowned king by the Pope, Urban VI. The inscriptions and the mount with its heraldic achievements, which were recorded by Gagnières in a coloured drawing datable to *c*. 1713 and are fully discussed by Lane who believed the mounts to be of German craftsmanship. When the mounts were lost is not precisely known, except that it must have been after 1822, when William Beckford of Fonthill Abbey had to sell his property in order to pay his debts; the mounts are mentioned in the sale catalogue and in contemporary documents. This astonishing pear-shaped vase with spreading mouth, a fairly common form, as we have already seen, had carved and incised decoration similar to that of the Toronto vase (Plate 3), but with a lotus scroll filling the central band. The decoration, however, goes far beyond this and the final result constitutes one of those ludicrous and elaborate experimental pieces which turn up at intervals all through the history of Chinese ceramic art.

[1] A. Lane, 'The Gagnières-Fonthill vase; a Chinese porcelain of about 1300', *Burlington Magazine*, 103, 1961, pp. 124–32.

The four lobed panels are cut into the body round the main band of carved decoration and in total disregard of the carved lotus scroll. Into the panels are set floral reliefs which have been pressed out in moulds and secured with plugs of clay at the back to the thin inner wall of the vase. As though this were insufficient as a display of the inappropriate, beaded relief bands and curlicues have similarly been added to the surface, with the same disregard for the existing carved and incised decoration. Nor is this the only example of the experimentalism of the time. Other examples are the vase with gilt mounts in the Victoria and Albert Museum[1] (Plate 7B), and there is a third one in the British Museum; both of these are cut down. The bottle in the Victoria and Albert Museum differs from the others in that the body is octagonal in horizontal cross-section, a form that has close connections with Near Eastern metalworking as well as with the native tradition in blue and white.

This experimentalism is extended at the same time in another direction which is equally remarkable, but which causes less of a shock to the sensibilities. During the early fourteenth century for instance there are stem-cups and bowls, many of them of stoutly moulded form, on which panels have been formed using the relief beading technique. Some of these panels vary in shape and size and hence in their appropriateness to the form of the vessel. They are sometimes given extra adornment by adding small relief elements in the panels. The stem-cup in the City Art Gallery at Bristol is an excellent example of this, with its small figures applied to each panel on the outside (Plate 8A). The beading on this cup continues into the inside and terminates in the centre under an applied relief prunus blossom, like that in the centre of the Cleveland Museum of Art's splendid cup with its freely modelled dragon handle (Plate 8B).

Other examples take this development a stage farther. In the Brundage Collection in San Francisco is a pair of vases in stands (Plate 9). These vases are of *mei-p'ing* form with somewhat elongated necks; the paired arrangement of the beaded relief panels alternates with applied slip decoration of lotus sprays alternating with phoenixes round the walls. The slip appears to have been roughly applied to conform broadly in outline with the proposed elements, and has then been tidied up with some careful tool work. The most elaborate and splendid example of this unusual style is the ewer at present on loan to the Chicago Art Institute (Plate 10). This fine specimen is of excellent quality of body and glaze, and the execution of the complex design is probably unsurpassed. The petal panels round the lower section of the body are not in this case carved, but laid on in slip

[1] Formerly in the collection of Baroness Cassel van Doorn.

which has been exceptionally well controlled in the ornamental treatment of the inner part. Slip has also been used for the bold phoenix decoration on the upper part of the body, and here the careful tooling of the edges and the incising of the details on the birds can be clearly seen. The boldly modelled scaly dragon handle and base of the spout, both in fact mould constructed, indicate a highly developed technique of moulding and great skill in the modelling of the details. Tying the spout to the neck is a well-shaped S-curve link, a feature which is fairly common at this time and may be found on temple vases like a small one in the Ashmolean Museum at Oxford, on which they serve as handles. Round the neck of the ewer is an angular meander of finely beaded relief. This meander ornament is common on a number of wares during the late thirteenth and all through the fourteenth century, and it serves to press home the close connection at this period between metalwork, from which it mainly derives, and ceramics.[1] The decoration of the neck, again in carefully controlled slip designs, appears once more to demonstrate a feature common in the period, of combining unrelated elements on the same surface. The cover, surmounted by a lion with one fore-paw raised to rest on a beribboned ball, may possibly be a later replacement. The character of both body and glaze differs noticeably from that of the ewer itself, although the animal in some respects is very close to the example, albeit of much larger size, on a pedestal in the Ashmolean Museum (Plate 11). The Ashmolean lion, evidently one of a pair, is likely to have been part of a set of Buddhist figures for a family altar or small shrine.

This brings us directly to the source of the peculiar pearl beading in relief as a part of the decoration. We are fortunate in being able to refer to the massive Buddhist figure in the Nelson Gallery in Kansas City, which is dated to either 1298 or 1299 (Plate 12). The figure, a Bodhisattva, is one of a number now known on which beading in relief has been used to represent the traditional necklaces and bracelets with which these saintly personages are usually adorned.[2] The application of sculptural concepts to ceramic figures of this size, 51·4 cm. in height, set the potters a number of problems, the chief of which is one of construction. The figure in this case is hollow, as one might expect, the body being of ch'ing-pai type, although the glaze has the marked tendency to opacity that qualifies the piece as an

---

[1] For the history of this motif see the author's *Metalwork and Chinese Ceramics*, 1972, pp. 17–18.

[2] J. Ayers: 'Buddhist porcelain figures of the Yüan Dynasty', *Victoria and Albert Museum Year Book*, 1969, gives a list of figures of this kind available at the time, but further figures have become known since the date of this article.

example of the transitional type. Damaged and imperfect in accomplishment, it nevertheless marks an interesting departure from the traditional materials of Buddhist sculpture and is an exciting new use of porcelain. In interpretation the figure follows very closely similar figures in bronze and in painted wood, and it fulfils its religious purpose at least as well. Other examples, more accomplished than this, are the Dresden figure first published by Ernst Zimmermann,[1] and those in the Rietberg and Metropolitan Museum (Plate 13) discussed by John Ayers at the Brundage Symposium on Oriental Art in 1966. Most of the best-known figures are large, about 46 or 51 cm. in height, though some are now so badly damaged that the original size can only be guessed at on the basis of the proportions of the parts that remain. A number of smaller figures are beginning to come to light, one good example of about 23 cm. having recently been acquired by the Victoria and Albert Museum. This is a very pleasing specimen, the details of the beading and relief ornament having been handled with restraint and care. The most elaborate, and perhaps the latest in the series on account of certain features in the upper part of the robe, is the figure tentatively identified as Manjuśri in the Metropolitan Museum (Plate 13). The left hand is a rather poor restoration, but in other respects the figure is complete and almost undamaged. In construction, it is like the Kansas figure in being hollow, and it has a strong central partition running up from the open roughly finished base; this partitioning strut serves to carry the considerable weight of the head and shoulders, while permitting adequate ventilation for the firing. The body material and the glaze, with its slightly matt appearance and bluish tone, brings this piece very close to the Shu-fu type, but like the Kansas figure it is probably best regarded as transitional white ware. The beading, much finer than on the other large figures, is exceptionally elaborate, so too is the robe with its 'cloud collar'-like lappets falling from the shoulders, down each arm and on the chest just beneath the raised left hand. 'Cloud collar' elements were to play an important part in the decoration of blue and white and copper red wares, but this is so far the only example of the use of this motif on any other ceramics in the period.[2]

---

[1] 'Eine Porzellanfigur aus der Yüanzeit in der Dresdener Porzellansammlung', *Ostasiatisher Zeitschrift*, 1937, pp. 143–4. Zimmermann identified it as Tê-hua ware from Fukien.

[2] The figure in the Victoria and Albert Museum has what are better described as lappets. These occur only on the shoulder; the Metropolitan Museum example has the element falling also in front. The absence of the fourth part on the back is probably to be explained by the fact that the figure was intended to be viewed frontally, so the labour of executing this piece of modelling could reasonably be avoided.

These large white figures of Buddhist deities are not the only figures found in the *ch'ing-pai* tradition. Recently, in the Philippines especially, a number of small figures of Lohans and Taoist immortals have been found, suggesting that the production of this type was well developed and may have continued for several decades. These smaller figures, mostly 15 to 30 cm. in height, vary greatly in quality and style. The problem of dating them is difficult for we only have the Kansas figure to work from at present, but it would seem reasonable to suppose that they were made from about 1290 onwards, with the New York figure lying relatively late in the sequence, perhaps even as late as the end of the first quarter of the fourteenth century, if we relate them to the large blue and white and copper red wine jars discussed in the following chapter.[1] The relationship between these and the Fonthill type vases is very close. The absence of securely dated specimens is always a handicap, and in this case to pursue the question of dating on the basis of style, or for that matter on the basis of this very peculiar technique, is too hazardous to attempt. Nevertheless the tendency of the potters to move away from the *ch'ing-pai* towards a stouter ware with a thicker, more opaque glaze is suggestive support for relatively later dating for the Manjuśri figure and the Fonthill vase, as well as linking them with the blue and white and copper red jars.

The first firm date we have in the fourteenth century for white porcelain is 1328, a transitional white ware dish in the David Foundation (Plates 14A, B). This dish, constructed on a mould, is not only a new shape in white ware but also in the total repertory of Jao-chou. It has a glaze that clearly foreshadows Shu-fu. The rounded sides and straight rim are quite unlike any other wares up to this time in the *ch'ing-pai* stream; so, too, is the wide unglazed base. Even the moulded decoration of phoenixes among clouds is different and more massive in treatment, foreshadowing other moulded dishes with dragons round the sides, with either a copper red or a cobalt blue glaze, both types generally attributed to the second half of the century. The dish is somewhat thinner than these later pieces, and although the unglazed base is rough, the foot-ring is neatly finished. The four-character mark reading *T'ien-shun nien tsao*, 'Made in the T'ien-shun period', is located on the front just outside the central field and is barely visible to the naked eye. It was originally published as being in slip relief,[2] but was later revealed under the microscope at high power to have been incised into the paste before glazing. The glaze itself, slightly bluish in tone, is marred here and there by ferruginous impurities and tends to lie in a thickened welt on both sides of the

---

[1] See below, p. 32.

[2] M. Medley, 'A T'ien-shun saucer', *Archives of Asian Art*, XXI, 1967–68, pp. 67–9.

mouth-rim, a feature that is especially characteristic of Shu-fu wares, and is also a feature noted by Sung Mang-chou in his note on a white saucer with moulded decoration of the Eight Buddhist Emblems with a moulded inscription of the name of the shrine for which it was made.[1] This specimen, now in the Palace Museum in Peking is dated by Sung on literary and historical evidence after 1328, the date when the sacrificial office, the name of which is inscribed on the piece, was established. The dish discussed by Sung is interesting because he states that in fifty years' experience he has only been able to record three examples of this type, all of the same size and almost certainly all from the same mould. Of the other two, one was handed to Peking University and the other, according to him, has disappeared. It seems more than likely, however, that the third example is the one recently acquired by the Victoria and Albert Museum (Plates 15A, B). If this is the case, we have in this piece a type later in date than the David Foundation one and different in glaze in as much as this is thicker, more opaque and very white and glassy.

From this point on, white wares seem to have developed in two distinctly different ways. In one direction the move was towards a rather well-finished relatively thin type with moulded decoration, sometimes with incising, and usually with a glazed base and a narrow well-trimmed foot-ring, of which the Ashmolean dish is representative (Plates 16A, B). And in the other direction the move was towards a bold strong form with unglazed base and square-cut foot-ring of comparatively small diameter, and a true Shu-fu glaze, thick and opaque, tending to bluish tone (Plates 18A, B).

Belonging to the first type, the Ashmolean Museum dish displays the special qualities to be associated with this slightly divergent type. Round the sides is a chrysanthemum scroll with four flowers, two each of different kinds, and in the centre is a single incised lotus flower on a curving stem. Like the T'ien-shun dish this one shows ferruginous impurities in the white slightly opaque glaze, which thickens a little in places round the outside of the rim. The base is carefully treated so that the glaze reaches half-way down the inner side of the foot-ring. The style of the decoration and the quality of the glaze bears a close resemblance to a number of blue and white stem-cups, with similar decoration inside, and so should perhaps be dated to the second quarter of the fourteenth century. The dish is technically more advanced than the 1328 one in that the glaze is better controlled and the body somewhat cleaner. The same comment

[1] 'Yüan luan-pai yu yin-hua yün-lung pa-pao p'an' ('A moulded white glazed dish of the Yüan period with dragons in clouds and the eight emblems'), Wên-wu, 1963, No. 1, pp. 25–6.

can probably be made of the extremely sophisticated plate with flattened foliate rim and moulded decoration of two dragons chasing pearls, which was found together with another foliate rimmed vessel, a bowl, and some blue and white pieces in the Pao-ting hoard in 1964 from Hopei[1] (Plate 17).

This remarkable find at first sight ought to help a great deal towards dating the fourteenth-century wares, but unfortunately it was only a hoard, cached away without any material in other media. There were no associations and so no firm conclusions to be drawn beyond the likelihood that none of the blue and white, on the basis of our present chronology, was later than about 1360, and that some of it would seem to belong to the second quarter of the century. With this in mind, the plate, together with the mechanical handling of the form, may date from anywhere within this period from 1330 to 1360. The inclination is to place it very shortly before the middle of the century, on account of the dragons which resemble those on the inside of the blue and white stem-cups, generally accepted as belonging to the earlier stratum of blue and white, and thus before 1351, the first landmark in the development of the blue and white.

The Shu-fu wares, allied to the transitional white type and probably developing from them, perhaps not much before the middle of the fourteenth century, are stoutly made and generally well-finished, with a very squarely cut rather thick foot-ring. The base, usually though not invariably unglazed, often comes to a slight nipple-like point at the centre. The forms are limited in their range, but always with a foot-ring the diameter of which is rather small in proportion to the whole in both height and diameter. The bowls are of two types, one with rounded sides and everted rim (Plates 18A, B) and the other with almost straight slightly flaring sides, contracted at a sharp angle to the small foot (Plates 19A, B). Both types have moulded floral decoration round the wall and may have the double *vajra*, or thunderbolt, in the centre. Some examples have the two characters *shu* and *fu* written in slip facing each other across the centre from their place on the inner wall, but these characters on such bowls may often be omitted. The characters when they appear are often applied quite arbitrarily and without regard to the decoration, cutting across it so as to disfigure it and break the rhythm of the flower scroll. On both these types of bowl the outside is plain.

Apart from these pieces, there is a large series of bowls, much more varied in size, but still rather limited in decoration. They fall broadly into two groups, those with straight rim and those with slightly

---

[1] '*Pao-ting shih fa-hsien i-p'i Yüan-tai tz'ŭ-ch'i*' ('Yüan dynasty porcelain discovered at Pao-ting'), *Wên-wu*, 1965, No. 2, pp. 17–18, 22. See below.

everted rim. Many, like the saucers, are decorated with stylized lotus scroll in moulded relief. Others also with moulded decoration, have geese in flight among clouds, bordered above by a narrow wave band. The pattern of waves is sometimes rather imperfectly accepted from the mould, and is perhaps an indication either of poor craftsmanship or a lack of plasticity in the porcelain clay. All the larger bowls carry the characters *shu* and *fu* in slip, and some of them have incised petal panels on the outside radiating from the foot-ring, which as with the saucers is rather thick. This large group of bowls is always strongly constructed, and those with the incised petal panels seem to belong to the later years of the fourteenth century, continuing into the early part of the Ming dynasty, for they link up with bowls of similar size and shape, and in general characteristics of body and glaze, that are moulded on the inside with a design of chrysanthemum petals arranged in concentric bands. Forms other than these bowl and saucer shapes are much less common, but a number of small tripods, based on bronze forms, like that in the Eugene Bernat Collection (Plate 20A) turn up occasionally. There are too a few spouted bowls, one of exceptionally fine quality being in the Malcolm Collection, on the inside of which there was once a gilt dragon (Plates 20B, C). The spouted bowls, however, are better known with underglaze blue or copper red decoration, and with a body closer in type to *ch'ing-pai*.

The body and glaze characteristics of the whole of this type of ware which we term Shu-fu are remarkably consistent. The well-levigated body is very dense, fine-grained and white, usually burning slightly orange where it is exposed, especially along the line where the glaze ends on the outside of the foot-ring. The glaze, moderately thick, is noticeably more opaque than the transitional white type, and is very often matt in appearance. The colour varies with a bluish or greenish tinge, and in a few cases may even incline to grey; this is mainly a firing variation and is not a fundamental difference that has to be distinguished. One constant feature, already mentioned in connection with the T'ien-shun dish, is the tendency for the glaze to thicken in a slight welt on either side of the mouth rim; sometimes the glaze may run down from the rim more thickly in one or two places. A handsome and justly admired ware, the date of its introduction still evades us, as does the real meaning of the term Shu-fu, and in its turn the date of its transformation into the Ming tradition. The earliest recorded use of the term in connection with ceramic ware occurs in the *Ko-ku yao-lun*, an antiquarian handbook by Ts'ao Chao, with a preface dated 1388. Whether research in the future will reveal an earlier use of the term remains to be seen, or even the real meaning of the term in relation to porcelain; it only occurs on white wares.

THE WHITE WARES OF JAO-CHOU

The Shu-fu type used always to be thought to have been confined to the Chinese mainland, but this has now been shown to be untrue. Some nice examples of smaller bowls and dishes have recently been recovered from excavations in the Philippines, and although none of these has so far borne the two distinguishing characters, a few have been of the highest quality. The possibility that the Chinese sold off wasters inevitably comes to mind. Some of the pieces, however, display features that associate them more with the transitional type, and one would perhaps classify them as such were it not for the method of construction and the style of the decoration. The Philippine finds include a considerable range of jars, or jarlets, as they are appropriately called on account of their small size. These are usually rounded globular objects, or slightly elongated into a dumpy ovoid form, sometimes fluted, sometimes decorated with beaded relief; most are constructed in two or three parts, each moulded and then luted together. Many have small cylindrical loops at the junction of the shoulder and neck. The body material is varied, some of it falling neatly into the *ch'ing-pai* category, some transitional in type and some closer to the Shu-fu in its fineness and density, and it often burns a pale orange tone where it is exposed in the firing. The glaze may be thin, translucent and slightly blue in tone, as is characteristic of the *ch'ing-pai*, or it may be thicker and opaque, and sometimes even have a matt surface like the general run of Shu-fu. Because of these wide variations in the character of the wares, dating is particularly difficult to determine. It may also be that a number of different kilns were involved in producing a range of white wares and that they continued in operation for the general market over a long period with little or no change of form because the mass-production techniques by their very nature tended to discourage it. A similar confusing situation is to be found when we turn to other white wares of a more popular character, wares that include a complex series of ewers, of which the double gourd form and the roughly pear-shaped ewer of rectangular cross section are the most common. The gourd ewers, of which fairly large numbers have been found in the Philippines in recent years, are built up of four roughly hemispherical parts luted together one on top of another, with a spout added on one side and either a simple strap handle, or a freely modelled dragon handle on the other. These have not so far been found with applied or moulded decoration, but they do include a number of iron-spotted examples as well as some with either underglaze blue or copper red decoration.[1]

[1] L. and C. Locsin, *Oriental Ceramics discovered in the Philippines*, Plates 77–87, and J. Addis, 'Chinese porcelain found in the Philippines', *T.O.C.S.*, 37, 1967–69, Plates 39, 40 and 42.

The second type, also found in the Philippines, is of rectangular cross section. This is a more complicated type in that the surfaces all carry moulded decoration, which is at its most splendid on the two larger surfaces between the spout and handle (Plate 21A). Such ewers are luted together vertically up the short sides, the joint being largely camouflaged by the attachment of the spout and handle. The larger side, as in the example illustrated, is characteristically decorated with a major field, in this case composed of an elaborate multi-lobed panel composed of trefoil elements, enclosing a naturalistic design, and bordered above and below by narrow horizontal scrolling bands, a concept of surface and its organization common throughout the fourteenth century and found at every level of production. There is also a third type of ewer, again found in the Philippines, which is round and dumpy like a sauce pot, with a short curving spout. This is luted together horizontally in two main parts with little attempt to conceal the join, indeed it is almost emphasized in the example from the Locsin Collection (Plate 21B) by the attractive rather sharply defined leafy scroll running round both upper and lower parts.

A technical point of some interest is that nearly all these small pieces, whatever their shape, are, if made in moulds, taken from them without any trimming up. This is especially to be noticed in the base and foot, the inner wall of which is a little rough with no indication of any attempt at neat finishing. This is the case with the ewer illustrated in Plate 21B. If there is only a vestige of a foot-ring, as occasionally happens, it is a feature included in the mould and there is never any sign of subsequent tooling. The same practice seems to have been followed at other kilns producing similar shaped wares, such as those making Lung-ch'üan type celadons and those in Fukien making white wares.

In describing the white porcelains of Jao-chou in the Yüan period from the late thirteenth century to the end of the fourteenth century the main problem is, and is likely to remain, that of the variety of bodies and glazes. The likelihood of the earlier types with lightweight bodies and translucent glazes surviving all through the period and even into the early years of the Ming dynasty cannot be wholly discounted; it is extremely probable, especially at outlying kilns engaged on production for the less demanding sectors of the market, and even the export market. Until much more archaeological evidence is available upon which to base closer dating, our conceptions of the chronology of the white wares must to a large extent remain somewhat speculative, but the broad pattern that leads on into the fifteenth century is nevertheless clearly to be discerned.

3

UNDERGLAZE BLUE AND
COPPER RED DECORATED WARES

Of all the many and interesting problems relating to blue and white
porcelain production in China, perhaps the most intriguing, and still
the farthest from being satisfactorily resolved, is that of the date of the
introduction of cobalt blue for use on porcelain. Despite long and
diligent research the solution continues to evade us, little progress
having been made since the first major assaults carried out on the
subject by Sir Harry Garner[1] and John Pope.[2] Pope, who studied the
literary evidence with some care, and examined the archaeological
evidence, as well as the lack of it, with a highly critical eye, made the
position clear that there was no sound basis for accepting a Sung date
for this innovation,[3] but was too cautious to do more than hint at a
fourteenth-century date. Garner more boldly writes, 'Although the
exact date at which the Chinese first made blue and white cannot yet
be ascertained, the evidence that we have at present suggests that
manufacture was not started much before the beginning of the fourteenth century.'[4]

Since 1954 much new material has become available, but there is
still no evidence to support the old view, cautiously dismissed by
Pope, that blue and white began as early as the Sung dynasty, rather
the reverse. The weight of the evidence, much of it negative it is
true, suggests that the date should be sought in the first half of the
fourteenth century. It is particularly significant that Chiang Ch'i in
his *T'ao-ch'i lüeh* ('Appendix to the Ceramic Records')[5] makes no

[1] *Oriental Blue and White*, 1954., 2nd edn., 1964, 3rd edn., 1970.
[2] *Fourteenth century blue and white: a group of Chinese porcelains in the
Topkapu Sarayi Müzesi, Istanbul*, Freer Gallery of Art, Occasional Papers, Vol. II,
No. 1, Washington, 1952. Abbreviated to *Topkapu Sarayi. Chinese porcelains
from the Ardebil Shrine*, Washington, 1956. Abbreviated to *Ardebil*.
[3] *Ardebil*, p. 38.
[4] *Oriental Blue and White*, p. 2; but see also the Preface to 2nd edn., 1964, p. xvi.
[5] See above, p. 7.

mention of it. Careful study of the text and the terms, many of them technical, makes it clear that he went to a lot of trouble to try and understand the industry as it then was, and it seems inconceivable that he should not have mentioned cobalt blue, which in ceramics yields such brilliant effects and a splendour so much at variance with the traditional conceptions of ceramic decoration. It is also suggestive that if the blue pigment were being imported, which we know all fourteenth-century cobalt to have been, that it should not have been mentioned on this account. It was the only colouring pigment so far as we know which came from abroad, and only, at this time, from abroad. This would have been of some importance to the managers of the kilns and would almost certainly have been a fact known to the craftsmen. As the *T'ao-ch'i lüeh* was written in 1322 and there are in it these two rather significant omissions, it is not beyond the bounds of possibility that painting in cobalt blue did not begin before about the end of the first quarter of the fourteenth century; it may in fact have started even later, though in view of the Fonthill vase and the technically related *kuan* wine-jars (Colour Plate B), of which three are now known, it cannot have started very long after, and the inclination would be to set the introduction between 1322 and 1330. When we survey the whole body of material for the fourteenth-century develop-ment, this still gives the decorators and the kiln masters ample time to achieve the degree of control that is displayed with such spectacular effect in the David Foundation vases of 1351, our first and only securely dated fourteenth-century examples (Plate 24).

If we accept that cobalt blue was introduced in the early part of the second quarter of the fourteenth century, we must then turn to the consideration of how this came about, what the motivation was that sparked off this revolutionary change in artistic direction, which was initially condemned as 'very vulgar'. There can be no doubt that the conditions both socially and economically were ripe for change, for although in late Southern Sung times the stimulus given to foreign trade was quite marked, it was to be greatly increased under the Mongols. During the thirteenth century there had already been a change in the focus of foreign trade which shifted north from Canton to Ch'üan-chou (Marco Polo's Zayton) and from this port, so much closer to the centres of ceramic production, the trade in celadons already well established was to be supplemented in the fourteenth century by the blue and white, both achieving bulk proportions. It was at Ch'üan-chou where most of the Persian and Arab merchants were established and where the commercial lingua franca was Persian. The great wealth of many of the merchants and shipping masters meant that the inflow of foreign goods, particularly textiles and metalwork, was likely to exert an influence on the Chinese, whose major export apart from silk was ceramics. The ceramic wares, both the Lung-ch'üan celadons and the *ch'ing-pai* of Kiangsi, had long been admired in the Islamic west for their hardness and beauty of form as the finds of great quantities of these materials in the refuse heaps of Fostat demonstrate. The wares had a strength and durability far greater than anything being currently produced in Islam, where the ceramics were comparatively low-fired, fragile and rather soft-glazed. Thus the many foreign merchants, both resident and visiting, would have ample opportunity with the help of their own financial backing to stimulate the Chinese to satisfy a desire for more colourful and decorative products. There seems no doubt in these circumstances that they were instrumental in introducing the arsenide of cobalt, probably in a prepared smalt form, to the potters of Jao-chou, where the financial stringency in the years following the Mongol conquest had forced a change in the organization of the kilns. In Southern Sung times most of these had been small and privately owned, but after the conquest great numbers were taken over by commerical syndicates, a point stressed by Chiang Ch'i in his *T'ao-ch'i lüeh*.[1] The injection of capital by merchants would inevitably favour changes, and the merchants would certainly have contacts far outside the area and with the foreign communities at Ch'üan-chou; conditions would thus be established wholly beneficial for the introduction of new ideas. There is no doubt that this is precisely what occurred and that blue and white was initially produced to satisfy foreign demand in both forms and decorations. It is of some significance that the greater proportion of surviving fourteenth-century material consists of large pieces, very few of which have been found in China. Such smaller pieces as have been recovered in China have been for the most part vessels intended for temple use, unsuitable for the foreign market and probably made for local patrons in the south.[2]

In the Near East cobalt had been used for the decoration of earthenware as early perhaps as the Abbāsid period in the late tenth or eleventh century, and was certainly used in the thirteenth century. In the earliest examples the blue was used in combination with a tin glaze, which tended to inhibit the running of the pigment, but later the cobalt was used on an artificially constituted body, that owed but little to Chinese influence, and was then used with a transparent alkaline glaze, the decorative effects often being marred by flooding of the cobalt, which is itself a flux, in the clear glaze. This could not

---

[1] *Fu-liang hsien chih*, Ch. 4, f. 46b, et seq., 1683 edn.
[2] The almost complete absence of small bowls, small dishes and plates is very significant in this respect.

occur so easily in a tin glaze, since the tin oxide forms an insoluble precipitate in the glaze. Perhaps it was on account of this problem of achieving a stability of outline that some merchants had the wit to think of presenting the problem to the Chinese, from whom in the Near East so much had already been learned. That the pigment was introduced to the Chinese in a prepared state, or at least partly prepared, seems more than likely. It would otherwise have been difficult to have achieved satisfactory results. It is clear too that the pigment entered China by way of the sea-route from the Persian Gulf, passing down to Sumatra, probably being trans-shipped at Acheh or Pisé at the northern tip of the island, which at this time was the most thriving port where Chinese, Persians and Arabs had resident communities of merchants. The other possible centre was San-fo-chi (Sri Vijaya), identified with Palembang on the east coast of Sumatra. This brings up the inevitable question of the names the Chinese gave to cobalt, and it may perhaps be as well to clear up a persistent misunderstanding. The names found most commonly before the sixteenth century are all three-syllable names beginning *Su* or *Sa*, *Sumali* being perhaps one of the most usual. It is this name which mistakenly gave rise to the idea that the blue came from Sumatra, and that the word itself meant Sumatra. In fact the Chinese did not at this time, or in the fifteenth century, name Sumatra as such. They did however use the name *Su-mên-ta-li*, but only to identify Sri Vijaya and its capital Palembang.[1] It is apparent that the names *Su-ma-li*, *Su-ma-ni*, *Su-ni-po* and *Sa-po-ni* and so on are phonetic approximations of the name of cobalt in another language, the Chinese variations probably being accounted for by dialect differences. The problem is a linguistic one and not primarily a geographical one. The important point is that all the blue was imported during the fourteenth century by the sea-route, and it was not until the sixteenth century that the term *hui-ch'ing* or *hui-hui-ch'ing*, usually translated as 'Muhammadan blue', was introduced. This blue was also imported, but some of it came overland, a distinction commented on in *Shui-pu pei-k'ao*,[2] where it is explained that *hui-ch'ing* came from Samarkand and other places, and was another name also for *Su-ma-li* blue which came from Java (*sic*). These names are distinct from those which the Chinese gave to their native blue, most commonly referred to as *shih-ch'ing*, 'stone blue'.

[1] San-fo-chi was the fourteenth-century name, but it seems to have been changed about the end of the century, after the Mongol defeat by the Ming, to Su-mên-ta-li, a name which persisted in a number of variant forms all through the Ming dynasty.

[2] This rare text, printed and issued in the Wan-li period at the end of the sixteenth century, was an *aide-mémoire* for clerks in the Water Transport Section of the Kung-pu, Board of Public Works. On cobalt see Ch. 6, f. 15v.

UNDERGLAZE BLUE, COPPER RED DECORATED WARES

Wherever the pigment came from and whatever method was used in its preparation, it was employed in painting in the same way. It was applied, as it normally is today, directly to the body. This inhibits its tendency, as a flux, to run causing unsightly blurring of the decoration, because the colour is 'fixed' to a certain extent by sinking slightly into the body. The pigment is very strong, contaminates other materials surprisingly easily, and has to be carefully diluted; failure to dilute sufficiently results in the excess cobalt rising through the glaze during the firing and then oxidizing to black or sometimes reddish brown on the surface. The Chinese would seem to have mastered the technique of handling the material quite quickly and relatively few really primitive pieces can be recorded; one example of an early stage is perhaps represented by a small plate in the David Foundation (Plate 22), which has a lightweight *ch'ing-pai* body and a glaze transitional between true *ch'ing-pai* and Shu-fu, not dissimilar to that on the moulded dish dated to 1328, discussed in the previous chapter.[1]

At this point a serious area of doubt is encountered, and it may be that many specimens which in the past have been thought to belong to the earliest stratum of blue and white, in fact continue over a comparatively long period if only because they satisfied a local need and thus survive today as a clearly distinguishable group. Examples of these may be the stem-cups, moulded inside and painted outside with dragons, and some of the bottle vases and small covered jars, each of which was perhaps made to satisfy a particular requirement of a less affluent section of the community than the wealthy foreign merchants and their Chinese commercial counterparts, who dealt mainly in the large and elaborately decorated dishes. If these small pieces fulfilled an essential function, as they must surely have done, the potters would have been economically short-sighted not to have kept the market going for as long as it would stand it. It may be found in the future that these three types, painted only in blue,[2] the bottle vases and the small covered jars, painted either in blue or in copper red, the former colour predominating, continued in local production over a fairly extended period. There is also some doubt, as the evidence stands at present, as to whether copper red preceded cobalt as a pigment, or whether both were introduced at about the same time. It would certainly seem to be true, however, that cobalt blue, the more stable and more easily controlled of the two pigments

[1] See p. 25 above.

[2] The only exception at present recorded is the Riesco stem-cup, now in the British Museum, but this seems to have been painted in a brown iron pigment, not copper.

won the greater favour at an early stage. Whatever the answers to these two problems may prove to be, copper red and cobalt blue were apparently first used on a *ch'ing-pai* type body, which was characterized by lightness of weight in relation to the size. The arguments seem to apply to the material excavated in the last ten years in the Philippines, where associated material is insufficiently related to give a sound basis for any constructive inference with regard to dating of blue and white or copper red. If we take up this problem of the ratio of the weight to size, a comparison of the *ch'ing-pai* vase, with its incised lotus decoration (Plate 3), with the David Foundation bottle, which has similar decoration somewhat unsuccessfully reserved against a band of copper red (Plate 23) and the Brundage Collection bottle with lotus decoration painted in red, is found to be instructive in this respect. All three pieces are of about the same date, in the early part of the fourteenth century at the latest. The nearest relatives in blue and white to these three are Mrs. Clark's dragon bottles (Plate 25) and the Umezawa bottle with figures (Plate 38A), which are both very similar in their proportions. These two vases are still very light in weight in comparison with their size, but it is also found that there appears to be a slight difference in the glaze, which is more viscous than is the case with the David Foundation copper red painted bottle, and is also a little less transparent, having more in common with the mainstream of blue and white as it was to be established in the rest of the fourteenth century. A similar variation may sometimes be seen in the Philippines material. One peculiarity about some of the bottles is their method of construction; it may be found that the foot-ring, which is relatively thick and deep has been luted on separately.[1] A similar series of variations are found in one specifically fourteenth-century shape, the spouted bowl, of which there are now quite a large number on record. The glaze on these varies from true *ch'ing-pai* through to Shu-fu, from a marvellous transparency to a thick dull opacity, sometimes undecorated, sometimes painted in red and sometimes in blue. In these, however, there is an added difference in that the body also varies in weight and in thickness. In view of these inconsistencies in body and glaze, and perhaps in methods of construction, we are faced with several possible answers, and at the moment no means of determining which is the right one. Either all these pieces are as early as they have so far been supposed, or they extend over a period and represent a particular kiln or group of kilns, or a number of kilns only loosely related, occupied in the production of this fairly limited range of wares for a specific market.

[1] J. Pope, 'Two Chinese porcelains from the Umezawa Collection', *Far Eastern Ceramic Bulletin*, 41, June 1959, pp. 15–22.

B. *Wine-jar in underglaze blue and red. Ht. 33 cm.*
Percival David Foundation

UNDERGLAZE BLUE, COPPER RED DECORATED WARES

Without excavated material it is unlikely that the solution can be found.

The fundamental revolution in taste under the Yüan that we best see exemplified in the blue and white had a useful technical antecedent. The way was opened for the elaborate style of decoration for which blue was particularly suitable, and which was so much desired in the Near East, by the introduction of the moulding techniques. These moulding techniques lent themselves naturally to complex repeating designs, such as are at first found in twelfth- and thirteenth-century Ting and *ch'ing-pai*, quite apart from the industrial advantage of mass production by mechanical means. The enrichment of surface found in the moulded *ch'ing-pai*, with its combinations of floral and animal or bird motifs was especially suitable to the lay-out of design in the blue decorated porcelains of Jao-chou. It was the use of colour, rather than the modulation of surface that was alien to the conservative Chinese taste, though wholly in keeping with the Near Eastern preference for complex enrichment of surface and elaboration of detail. The fact that the Mongol conquerors showed so little desire to exert aesthetic direction of the potteries did much to make it possible for the foreign influence to accelerate the revolution in decorative taste, a revolution that was only to be completed in the early fifteenth century under the Ming. The basic decorative schemes owed much to Islamic taste with its predilection for infinitely extensible two-dimensional designs and visually unaccented enrichment of surface.[1] Nevertheless the Chinese adhered firmly in detail to their own repertory of naturalistic, mainly floral motifs. The only motif not of Chinese origin was a type of panel, included under the general name of petal panel, which in fact derives from the Arabic *lāmalif*. It occurs in two forms, both of them quite distinct from the true petal panel, one of which may be seen on the Topkapu plate (Plate 29B) both in the centre and in the band just inside the floral scroll, and the other more elaborate form occurs on the Ardebil plate (Plate 29A) also at the centre.[2]

The largest and most important body of material that is available for study is to be found in such collections as those of Topkapu Seray and Ardebil, and among the many specimens originally manufactured for the foreign trade. Apart from the David vases, which were made for a Chinese temple, relatively few pieces in proportion to the estimated total output have been found in China, and the best of these, to be discussed below, belong mainly to the last quarter of the

[1] M. Medley, *Chinese ceramics and Islamic design*, p. 7.
[2] Ibid., p. 3 and Plate 1, figs. e and g.

fourteenth century. While it is not too difficult to group certain types and treatments of decoration into the decades following 1351 and the David vases, the problem of determining what led up to these important objects and of identifying specific examples faces us with almost insuperable difficulties, and the results of research and attempts to group certain pieces into this earlier period can only be speculative. Since the largest sample of blue and white wares consists of plates, the principles of dating blue and white generally have been based on the study of these.

The David vases of 1351 provide as it were a half-way stage in the great assortment of designs, and their salient features should be enumerated (Plate 24).[1] But first it should be noted that the form of the vases, rather ungainly, owes nothing in its origin to the ceramic medium; it derives directly from cast bronze, and bronze examples of precisely this form are still to be seen in both Chinese and Japanese temples. In the brilliant blue painting are found the majority of the important fourteenth-century decorative elements and they are treated with an assured skill which implies a reasonable lapse of time between the introduction of the cobalt pigment and the date of manufacture. The floral elements include the three most popular ones of the period. First there is the fluently painted peony scroll round the high foot, second there is a formalized lotus scroll on the shoulder, and third there is the chrysanthemum scroll round the mouth. All these are found on the plates, together with the dragon, the male and female phoenix (*fêng-huang*), clouds, lotus panels with emblems and the bold wave decorations. The only elements not found on the plates, but common on vases, is the band of plantain leaves round the upper half of the neck. The elephant-head handles from which the rings have been broken off, on either side of the neck, are a special adjunct of temple vases and thus cannot be expected to appear on plates. Finally it should be noted that the dragons have richly painted scales on the body and that the phoenixes also have fully painted plumage; as will be seen, this is one of the crucial features relating to the chronology.

But before turning to the objects themselves it is advisable to draw attention to certain general principles that are discernible with regard to style in the fourteenth century. Careful examination of a wide range of blue and white demonstrates the fact that many hands were involved not only in forming the objects themselves, but also in the decoration of the surfaces. Because many decorators were at work, it

[1] For details of the inscription which dates these vases, see *Illustrated Catalogue of Porcelains decorated in Underglaze Blue and Copper Red in the Percival David Foundation of Chinese Art*, London, 1963, p. 46, No. B613.

was inevitable that there should be a certain latitude in the lay-out of the designs and a somewhat variable competence in the treatment of detail, so much so that on some occasions a lack of unity resulted. It necessarily became a requirement therefore to subordinate individual preferences to the need for a common style. The emergence of the fully developed style is gradual, indeed almost imperceptible, and it is a movement towards a unity in which symmetry played an increasingly important part. The plates themselves, for instance, begin from asymmetry, which gives way numerically in terms of the foliations of the rim and the number of the flowers to a logically grounded symmetry and regularity based on a properly calculated surface, that was to open the way for the fifteenth-century style. Numerical consistency became the first need, and this was achieved soon after the middle of the fourteenth century. The second consistency is one in which symbolism plays an important role, and is best seen in the late fourteenth century after the end of Mongol domination, but still during the period when the style initiated under alien rule was achieving its logical end.[1]

This seems to demonstrate what appears to be an immutable law of stylistic development in the visual arts, that greater consistency should be sought, by whatever means, for its own sake. That exceptions should occur is inevitable, but the later date of some of the inconsistencies can usually be pin-pointed because of the association with elements recognized for other reasons to be a later introduction. Unfortunately this can also work the other way, with an element being temporarily introduced and then discarded as being unsatisfactory in the context, and only later being re-introduced and developed. It is at this point that a study based solely on stylistic criteria is liable to defeat its own ends, the more so as the subjective element of judgement becomes strong and may override the technological necessities. Fortunately in ceramic studies the technology of the potter's craft to some extent counterbalances the dangers of a stylistically based approach, and so long as we remain aware of the dangers, the general rules of stylistic development will stand us in good stead. In Chinese blue and white especially we are well served, for there is a progression in technique alongside that of style, in as much as the products of the potter change gradually from hand craftwork to mechanical methods of manufacture. This leads to the conclusion that the more mechanical the methods of production became, the

[1] My recent paper 'The Yüan-Ming transformation in blue and white and copper red porcelains' in *Ars Orientalis*, IX, 1973, pp. 89–101, in fact takes this last group as a transitional one, but the survival of certain motifs and their manner of treatment up to the end of the century seems to justify the above statement.

more symmetrical, and hence consistent, the decoration. With the foregoing in mind we can now give our attention to the large plates, so characteristic of the Yüan period, and see how this principle is worked out in practice.

The large plates, measuring about 36 cm. or more in diameter can be divided into two main types: those with bracket foliations to the flattened rim, and those with a plain circular rim. These in turn can be broken down into three chronological groups in the first type and four groups in the second. The technical methods used in the construction of the two classes differ, the second, straight rimmed class being the more easily mass-produced, and thus ultimately the more persistent form. Into the basic framework of the style of these two classes as it develops, it may be possible to fit other forms in their correct chronological succession. The common features of the plates are, of course, the wide flat base, deep and well-rounded well, or cavetto, and the flattening of the rim, and, irrespective of whether it is foliated or not, this may be slightly flanged at the edge. We will follow the progression of form and decoration first in the bracket-foliated type, since the earliest of these appear to precede the straight rimmed type and indeed seem to be antecedents of the David vases.

The type can be broken down broadly into three groups related in a chronological succession, though there is some overlap between the second and third group. In the first group we find the most primitive examples which are eccentric in almost every respect. There is complete inconsistency in the number of foliations, the number of flowers in the encircling flower scroll, in the orientation of the flowers themselves, the number of waves breaking on the rim and in the proportions of the elements within the area. At the same time most of the basic elements that are to persist all through the fourteenth century are prominent. These are the wave band, the peony, chrysanthemum and lotus, the 'cloud collar', vine, gourd, morning glory, bamboo and minor landscape elements, the petal panel, the *lāmalif* panel, the knobbed scroll and emblems; in addition there are two types of water elements. Some of these decorative motifs are illustrated in Plates 122–4. The phoenix is also introduced and probably, were there sufficient surviving examples, it would be found that the dragon as well was in use.

There are only four examples of this first group immediately available for study, of which the three illustrated present the salient features (Plates 26A and B, 27). The first two examples, each with thirteen bracket-foliations, surely a most awkward number to accommodate, introduce certain characteristic elements to be seen in a long succession of specimens. The most striking feature is that the peony scrolls round the well are reserved against a blue ground and that the leaves in each case are 'hatched', that is the veins have been painted in. This treatment is to be found on all the dishes with foliate rims, with only two exceptions,[1] and also on a large number of vases and jars. It will also be noticed that the peonies themselves are of different kinds. On the plate (Plate 26A) on which the peonies are in profile the outer petals will be seen to be close to the main structure and, so to speak 'closed', while on the Topkapu Seray example (Plate 26B) the outermost petals fall away into an 'open' position. This again is a persistent feature up to the end of the second chronological group. A third characteristic is found on the plate in Plate 26B, which is also seen fairly constantly in all types of vessel; this is the very strange treatment of one peony, on the left half (at about ten o'clock), the flower having been split in a freakish manner. This unusual handling may occur whether or not the leaves and petals of the flowers are of the 'hatched' variety, even in late examples. Finally the number of flowers, seven, is unusual, and although an attempt has been made to fit them into the surface, difficulties have been encountered and they are not equidistant all the way round. The suggestion can be made that eight flowers were originally intended, as often on the outside this does occur, but that there was insufficient surface on which to dispose this number on the inside. This is the most reasonable explanation, but the Los Angeles example (Plate 27) also suggests that while flower scrolls were acceptable both inside and outside and patterns of some kind existed from which the decorators worked, there was as yet no established rule for the arrangement and number, for on the Los Angeles dish, when it is reversed, it is found that there are seven lotus flowers on the outside scroll. The wave pattern, which was necessarily painted free-hand rarely fits precisely into the space allotted for it and small variation and occasionally an appearance of crowding is common; moreover there is no rule as to which way it should be painted, clockwise or counter-clockwise. The numerical irregularities indeed extend quite consistently to the waves and generally add up to an odd number, as a simple check will show. In the emblems used in the petal panels, too, there is at this stage a similar absence of consistency, Buddhist and Taoist ones being freely and indifferently combined for the decorative effect. The 'cloud collar' element although carried out in the same way, with one broad band confined by an inner and outer line, is not always evenly spaced out on the surface, as may be seen on the Los Angeles plate, where we have six of these

---

[1] The exceptions are one plate in the Victoria and Albert Museum, which has a cross-hatched background to the well, and a plate, No. 29.45 in *Ardebil*, both advanced late examples.

as against a central medallion enclosing eight panels with emblems.[1] It seems that at this early stage the Chinese had fairly clear ideas about the kinds of decoration and use of surface appropriate to the new pigment, and probably had rough patterns from which to work, but had not yet settled down to drawing designs out properly according to any particular system.

The second group of foliate rim dishes shows the next stage when some attempt at symmetry is made and a more consistent series is the result. The fact that the foliations, when of an even number, are fourteen is an advance in the right direction, albeit based on a very peculiar number. For all this the general effect is one of greater regularity and more refined treatment. Two examples from Ardebil serve to illustrate this development. For instance, that in Plate 28A, with fourteen foliations and fourteen central panels and paired phoenix in the centre, immediately impresses one by its firmly controlled design. The chrysanthemum scroll and the wreath of camellia, a new floral element, although of an uneven number, is compelling by the regularity of the orientation of the flowers. There is also a punctilious alternation of flower sprays and emblems in the panels. The whole is executed in reserve against a blue ground and enhanced by hatched leaves of both the chrysanthemum and the camellia scrolls. Another example from Ardebil (Plate 28B) is of interest because here again, although the unusual number of fourteen foliations occurs, the central field is calculated on the basis of six with a central medallion of six bracket-foliation type enclosed in a larger one with two supplementary lobes in each section, a rather more complex treatment. The centre is decorated with a remarkable scene of herons wading in a lotus pool reserved in white on blue, and in the framing area between this and the outer medallion are clouds similarly reserved. The clouds are so close in treatment to a fine plate in Topkapu Seray,[2] which has a sixteen-foliate rim that the two pieces are probably very closely related, the Topkapu Seray one having a dragon in the centre and a lotus scroll with spiked leaves in blue on white round the well. The lotus scroll in the well of the Ardebil specimen, reserved in white like the other early examples, has scrolling leaves similar to those that occur on the Los Angeles dish with 'cloud collar' elements. The lotus flowers themselves are now more developed and complex. Of special interest is the wave border, which is magnificently controlled and is notable for a peculiar triple plume which, as it were, kicks back against the main current, producing a choppy effect (as in Plate 30),

[1] The Los Angeles plate has the lowest number of foliations on the rim so far recorded. There are only eleven, even more difficult to control than thirteen.

[2] Pope, *Fourteenth century Blue and White*, Plate 13.

a feature to which we shall have occasion to return at a later stage.[1] This small group seems to lie between the first one and perhaps the David vases, or at any rate so nearly contemporary with the latter as to make fine distinctions virtually impossible. Very little separates them from the fully matured style associated with this foliate form which we have set into a third group, a group to persist for some while after the mid-century landmark of the David vases.

This third group is extremely sophisticated in treatment, being almost without exception regular and symmetrical in foliation, based on a systematic arrangement of eight flowers in the well[2] and also in the orientation of the flowers, which follow a strict series of patterns (Plates 29A, B, 30, 31), and there is great regularity in the proportion of elements within a given area. Indeed the treatment is now so unified that it would seem almost as though the draughtsmen making the designs worked out the problems of organization using properly squared paper and drawing instruments. Two examples will suffice to demonstrate this very advanced stage. The first (Plate 29A) from Ardebil, an admirably controlled example, which perhaps shows better than any other the influence of the Near East in the enrichment of surface, and the consequences of an arithmetical approach to the surface to be decorated. The other example from Topkapu Seray (Plate 29B) is similarly precise in handling, but the overall impression is one that constantly impresses itself as characteristic, especially in vases, of the breaking up of the surface into unrelated areas. With panels and 'cloud collar' motifs cheek-by-jowl with fluently executed flower scrolling and boldly painted wave patterns, this dish could only have been produced by the Chinese.

The process used in the production of these dishes is important, because the wheel could not have been used. On account of the foliate rim, the system adopted was that of twin moulds, one for the inside and one for the outside, the clay being squeezed under pressure so that in diameter, detail of the rim and in thickness, the pieces remain consistent. Earlier examples of moulding techniques such as those of Ting and *ch'ing-pai*, which were much smaller, were made mainly by using a wooden bat to beat the clay on to the mould. For large pieces of this kind such a practice was impracticable as it would have taken too long. After being removed from the moulds the dishes had the foot cut in the ordinary way, mainly so as to tidy up the base and make a proper foot-ring, since the moulding could not be sharp

---

[1] A characteristic also occurring in some Turkish examples from Isnik.

[2] There is only one exception, No. 29.49 in *Ardebil*, and this has nine flowers. It is an unusually large dish in diameter, and this may account for the extra flower, which perhaps was seen to suit the proportions better.

enough on its own to give a really clean edge. To this third group of moulded pieces belong a number of dishes with complicated moulded decoration, in addition to the ordinary blue and white painting. There are a number of such plates in Ardebil and Topkapu Seray and some also in other collections. Two are of particular interest because they show how the treatment of detail was varied when still using the same basic design. One of these in Topkapu Seray (Plate 30) shows a freely painted centre with pheasants in blue and white surrounded in the well by a flower scroll moulded in relief and reserved in white, except for a few details painted in on the flowers, against a blue ground. The wave band rim is punctuated by six-petalled florets carefully isolated by a blue outline, the florets being moulded. The other plate (Plate 31), in the British Museum, is from the same mould, with a differently treated central field, though similarly blue on white; the flowers in the well are left without additional detail touched in, and on the border the wave pattern is carried over the florets ignoring the relief altogether. Although the border reliefs are ignored the waves break eight times, quite evenly round the rim with its sixteen foliations. Characteristic of these rather elaborately moulded examples is the use of blue on white in the central field in place of the reserved treatment of the earlier ones. The well-known large plate, formerly in the Hobart Collection, now in the Fogg Museum of Art, is a fine example of a highly individual treatment, the piece with its one inscribed panel clearly having been made to special order.

Among these foliate rim plates it is remarkable to find that virtually all the decorated surfaces are in white against a blue ground. One important exception is the dish from the Sedgwick Collection (Plate 32A). This belongs to the third and last group of this large variety which seems to date from a little before mid century to some time after, perhaps as late as 1360. At this stage the straight rimmed plate made its appearance and has in common with the foliated type certain important motifs, as well as a few new ones, which are discussed below. The strong drawing and unusual disposition in the Sedgwick plate of the elements of fish and waterweed in the central field mark this specimen out from among the other foliate examples. In addition the diamond diaper border pattern is almost unique, it normally being found in the straight rimmed variety in place of the wave pattern. The carefully calculated arrangement of the spiky-leafed lotus scroll, which is of a type not often associated with the foliate rim plate, at least in the well, shows that this motif was already in general use on other examples, although the rather sparse distribution of the leaves as compared with the Ardebil piece, also with a fish in

44

the centre, suggests a slightly earlier date. The Sedgwick plate seems to be a connecting link between the foliate and the straight rimmed plates. Taken in conjunction with another plate, from the Ardebil collection (Plate 32B), this suggestion receives some support. Again the foliate rim plate, once more with blue on white decoration in the centre, this time of a lotus pool, with a blackberry lily border, blue on white, and a peony scroll of eight flowers symmetrically treated and reserved in white on a blue ground. The plate nevertheless introduces another variant that has close links with the straight rimmed family. The lotus pool is a very popular theme, sometimes with ducks included, which continues through the first two chronological groups of the straight rimmed type. The peony scroll, so characteristic of the foliate rim variety, has its nearest relative in the fine plate in Tokapu Seray (Plate 33A), which shares with the Ardebil one the blackberry lily border, though here with the added embellishment of pomegranate flowers. The peony scroll is of the 'open' flowered type, but painted in blue on white, with leaves free of hatching, features that are also found on the David vases. Similar to the David vases is the treatment of the kylin with shaded scales on the body, which may also be seen on the dragons. A third example of a plate with blackberry lily border is one illustrated by Pope in Ardebil (Plate 14). This, unlike the one illustrated here has a straight rim and in the centre a phoenix with shaded plumage similar to the scales of the kylin and the dragons; the decoration of the well, however, is a lotus scroll, which is stronger in handling and fills the space more comfortably than is the case in the Sedgwick plate. Two other straight rimmed plates fall into the same group; one is the phoenix-decorated example in Topkapu Seray (Plate 33B) and the other is the kylin one in the Ashmolean Museum. Both have a diamond diaper border, the Ashmolean one being more elaborate, and both having creatures with shaded scales. The lotus scrolls encircling the well however differ markedly; the Ashmolean one shows very strict alternation in the orientation of the flowers, while the Topkapu one has one 'full-faced' flower of a distinctive type between two of the outward turned profile flowers. There seems no reason to doubt that all these four dishes, together with the two typical foliate rim ones, date from about the middle of the century and very close to the David vases. Of all those plates the Ardebil one shown in Plate 32B is the only one on which an eight-flowered scroll survives.

A second group, chronologically slightly later, includes a limited range of designs which display a variation in individual treatment that makes every piece of interest in some way. The lotus pond is probably the commonest, with fish and waterweed coming second, with a series in which freely disposed landscape elements are dominant. A few examples occur with a dragon in the centre, or with a pair of phoenixes; in these the treatment of the scales and feathers is linear. In every case in this second group, the well is filled with lotus scroll, and the border with diamond diaper. The most usual decoration on the outside is again the lotus scroll. Probably the finest examples of the group are the brilliant and exceptionally well-painted plate with pheasants from the Sedgwick Collection, now in the Victoria and Albert Museum (Plate 34A), and one with rather a different lotus scroll, with landscape elements scattered with characteristic freedom in the central field (Plate 34B). The incisive, but somewhat less rugged treatment is particularly noticeable in this group, the quality of which is generally of an exceptionally high standard. The control of the firing is clearly very accomplished. The range in size is narrower than with the foliate rim group, lying mostly between 41 and 46 cm. in diameter, and because they were produced mechanically on a fast wheel using a template, the thickness is remarkably consistent.

The third group sees the introduction of three new elements and a more mechanical handling, as though a logical conclusion were within easy reach. The first new element is the classic scroll, which makes its appearance as a border motif in place of the diamond diaper. The second, also a border motif, is a water element which Pope describes as 'segments of concentric wave pattern'.[1] Both of these may be accompanied on the outside by 'lotus panels' which neatly cover the curvature. An unusual and perhaps unique example of this type is the large plate in the Yale Peabody Museum (Plate 35A). This has the added feature of a fungus scroll round the well and free landscape elements in the centre, which when compared with Plate 34A, shows less imaginative handling although the rocks are of the same family as those of the preceding plate.

It was at this point, during the period from about 1360 to 1375 that the unexpected occurred and two differing styles began to emerge that were to lead into the new fifteenth-century tradition. It was also at this stage that many of the designs began to be executed in exactly the same way irrespective of the colours, whether blue or copper red. Precisely the same designs may be seen in both colours not only on plates, but also on vases, ewers and bottles, as we shall see later. There are a number of new motifs which provide keys to this transformation and became the means of injecting new life into a manufacture that was becoming progressively more mechanical and stereotyped. At the same time the decoration of the central

[1] *Ardebil*, Plate 7.

panel attains in most instances a greater degree of symmetry than formerly.[1]

Three of these new motifs were the classic scroll, the fungus scroll and the S-form key-fret. The first two of these, which appear together on the plate in the Yale Peabody Collection (Plate 35A) is the first indication of the change. The classic scroll on the flattened rim with its curving, flexing and reflexing line with added curls was to become from now on an extremely popular motif, and was also to be subject to a number of variations. It may, in the later stages, appear in the knobbed form as on the rim of the plate in the Palace Museum Collection (Plate 37), or it may be reversed so that it appears reserved in white against a coloured ground, or in a more elaborate treatment still as a filler in Plate 36B between the four lappets, each of which encloses a flower of the four seasons. The S-form key-fret, a variant form of the squared spiral seen on the mouth-rim of the *kuan* in Plate 45B is rarely seen on plates, though it does occur on the one illustrated on Plate 37; it is, however, common on bowls and small plates to be discussed later. Also in some sense new is a sparsely leaved chrysanthemum scroll which is now reduced to a narrow band only suitable for a flattened rim; formerly its large scale was wholly appropriate for the filling of the well, a position it now rarely occupies and when it does is very different in character. Finally among the border designs there is a debased wave pattern which is used both on the front and on the back of the foliated plates.[2]

[1] It will not escape notice that I here present a view at variance with that expressed by John Addis, who argues for a wholly Yüan attribution for this group. While agreeing that the type described here can be broadly included in what is often referred to as Yüan, and so affirmed by Addis, the need for more precise dating is desirable. In his paper 'A group of underglaze red', *T.O.C.S.*, 31, 1958–59, pp. 15–37, Addis adduces arguments that on close examination weigh at least as strongly in favour of Ming as they do of Yüan, and the limited range of wares he discusses would in any case favour a fourteenth-century date. But if our aim is, as I believe it should be, to seek closer dating, then we should abandon dynastic names and resort perhaps at first to parts of centuries, and then as our knowledge improves, to decades. My main desire is to try and present a survey of developments that is not falsely fortified by a conception of dynastic and hence political barriers against continuous artistic evolution. As Arthur Lane pertinently stressed many years ago in a paper (*T.O.C.S.*, 22, 1946–47, pp. 19–30), stylistic changes do not occur neatly in accordance with those of politics. The seeds of any new style are sown many years before they mature into one to which one might attach a political label. The reverse is also true, that the final stages in the maturity of a specific style may lie in a later political period. It is solely on account of this latter aspect that the argument here presented is continued right to the end of the century. The more detailed examination of the problems of transition from fourteenth-century Yüan to fifteenth-century Ming is presented in my paper in *Ars Orientalis*, IX, 1973, pp. 89–101.

[2] Jean Gordon Lee, 'Ming blue and white', *Philadelphia Museum Bulletin* No. 223, 1949, No. 20.

The introduction of the flowers of the four seasons is an important innovation. Up to this time the peony and chrysanthemum had been popular, but the symbolic associations has not been stressed; now they are joined by the pomegranate and camellia and are to be ordered in their proper sequence of peony, pomegranate, chrysanthemum and camellia and were to continue throughout the Ming dynasty. Sometimes the flowers are used as single sprays, as in the lappets already mentioned in connexion with Plate 36B, and in the well of the plate (Plate 37), where the motifs are repeated six times, and sometimes as a continuous scroll, but a favourite treatment is their free disposition as a series of rather large extended sprays, each with several flowers; they are then arranged round either the outside or the inside of the well and occasionally both, or as in the case of Plate 36A, round a small central medallion. In such cases as this last the decoration round the outside may be a peony or chrysanthemum scroll, or, again a new motif, a rather complex lotus scroll of the type seen in Plates 36A and B.

The change in style is nowhere more marked than in the central field, in which in many cases the use of flowering sprays, usually peonies, but also chrysanthemums, spring from a base line, sometimes with three distinct branches, but always in a more or less symmetrical arrangement and rather large in scale (Plates 35B and 37). The three examples illustrated by Sun Ying-chou in his article on Yüan, Ming and Ch'ing porcelain[1] seem clear evidence of this final stage, although he prefers an attribution to Yüan. Two of the pieces are painted in copper red and the third in blue. In the same category may be included some monumental plates from the Palace Museum Collection in Taiwan. Two of these (Plates 36A, B) in blue and white have a chrysanthemum scroll border on the flattened rim, characterized by a weakly painted and sparingly distributed leaf, a feature especially noticeable on Plate 36B. Both have the complex lotus scroll in the well and the flowers of the four seasons round the outside with a narrow band of lotus panelling below this based on the foot-ring. In the central field on one the 'cloud collar' motif is reduced to a series of lappets, each enclosing a spray of one of the flowers of the four seasons, with a small central medallion of a single lotus plant in a pool, the survivor of the old lotus plant and pond motif. Acting as a filler between the points of the lappets is the knobbed scrolling element meticulously repeated. In the centre of the other example (Plate 36A) the lotus plant and pool again occurs in the small central medallion, but this time is encircled by extended sprays of the flowers of the four seasons. The whole treatment of the central field has thus,

[1] Wên-wu, 1966, No. 3, p. 56, Figures 26–9.

although somewhat varied, become much more systematized in the organization of space.

Large bowls, straight at the rim, were introduced at this time with decoration very similar to that found on the large plates. One feature of the bowls, however, is a modified form of the 'cloud collar', such as is rarely found on the plates. It appears with four, six or even eight points constituting a dominant central medallion framing combinations of plant forms, generally bamboo and fungus, growing from a rock-strewn base line.[1] Nearly all the large bowls have a key-fret border round the central field and this is repeated round the foot-ring, a feature only found in plates of the very large bracket foliated type in which the foliations are carried right down into the foot-ring.

These massive plates with bracket foliations extending from the rim, down the well and including the foot-ring mark the final stage of the fourteenth-century development and are in some ways the most sophisticated examples of the potter's art in the whole period. Two of these, one in a private collection in Japan and the other in the Palace Museum, Taiwan (Plate 37) demonstrate not only the remarkable handling of design, but also an extremely advanced technical skill, for the foliations are perfectly aligned from the rim to the foot and even to the inner edge of the foot-ring. This is the clearest possible evidence of the use of twin moulds. The unglazed base of each plate has been carefully rubbed smooth after removal from the moulds and then wiped. In the Palace Museum plate the rim is filled with an elaborate classic scroll, while in each flute of the well is a flower spray with a band of key-fret above and below. The centre is dominated by a triple spray of peony. On the outside, following the same system as in the well, a flower spray of one or other of the flowers of the four seasons fill each lobe of the bracket foliation.

The other examples in this group, while conforming to the same general pattern, are somewhat less elaborate in as much as the foot-ring remains a true ring omitting the foliations, and the flower sprays are reduced to half the number and to a single species, which is repeated all the way round. The border patterns are in one case a fungus scroll on the upper side and a debased wave pattern on the underside. This wave pattern occurs on both surfaces of the Palace Museum example.

It is this final type of the fourth group, with either a straight or foliate rim, that leads directly into the fifteenth-century style, the Ming style, with which we have been for so much longer familiar.

[1] S. Jenyns, 'The Chinese porcelain in the Topkapu Seray', *T.O.C.S.*, Vol. 36, 1964–66, Plate 45b; also J. Addis, 'A group of underglaze red: a postscript', same volume, Plates 84a and b.

In the overall pattern of the seven groups described here, we have to fit all the other vessels, the jars, ewers, vases, bottles and bowls. The bowls are in a noticeable minority as compared, for instance, with the *mei-p'ing* vase; perhaps Shu-fu and celadon were preferred for this form, although recently there have been indications that there was a good market for them; fragments of bowls have been found at Fostat and whole pieces in the vicinity of Damascus.

It may be convenient at this point to summarize the scheme adopted here and to each group attach an approximate dating bracket, which, it must be emphasized, is quite tentative and may easily be contradicted and perhaps convincingly argued against; it will undoubtedly have to undergo some revision in the future as more evidence becomes available. It has, however, seemed right to make some attempt at a systematic chronological scheme, which may be set out here.

The two main classes of plate are first, the foliate rim type, and the second the straight rimmed type. The first class can be set out in the following three chronologically arranged groups:

(1) Completely irregular as regards foliations, the number of 'breaking waves', flowers in the scroll, the orientation of the flowers, and no regularly maintained series of proportions within a given area. To this group a dating range of 1330–40 might be given.
(2) An intermediate group in which there is a greater degree of regularity in any one of the sectors of form and design. This group appears to cover a short period from about 1340 to 1345.
(3) The most advanced group, which is almost universally regular and symmetrical in the main elements of forms and design. This can be dated as starting about 1345 and may continue to 1355, but might perhaps persist until about 1360.

The second class, of straight rimmed plates, may be set out in four groups, and into the fourth group the foliate rim is re-introduced in a slightly different form, in as much as there is no flange at the edge and the foliations are carried down the well.

(1) This group incorporates certain elements and techniques occurring already in Group 3 of the foliate type, such as the use of shaded scales and feathers, the blackberry lily scroll border and the practice of reserving the decoration in white against a blue ground. These pieces may be dated contemporary with Group 3 above, that is to 1345 to about 1355.
(2) Persistent use of the lotus scroll in the well, with landscape elements in the centre and a diamond diaper border. On the

outside of the well the lotus scroll is most usual. This group can be dated from about 1355 to perhaps as late as 1365.

(3) The introduction of the classic scroll border, and of segmented wave elements in the same context, and the use of petal panels on the outside of the well. These features combine with a very precise lay-out of the decoration of the well and the appearance of the fungus scroll. This group may overlap a little in date with the previous one and cover a period from as early as 1360 until about 1370, thus bridging the dynastic change from Yüan to Ming.

(4) The final group includes an elaborate classic scroll border, sometimes reserved in white on either a red or a blue ground, the fungus scroll, an emaciated chrysanthemum scroll and the S-form key-fet. The introduction of the flowers of the four seasons, either in the form of single flower sprays or in the form of a continuous scroll, is a new feature. The plate with foliated rim, which had been allowed to lapse, is re-introduced, with the foliations extending down the well and, in a few examples, right down to include the foot-ring, In these plates individual sprays, either of a single species of flower or of the flowers of the four seasons are used. The 'cloud collar' is another re-introduction, but now often reduced to a set of four lappets, and is used not only on plates, but also on the very large bowls with straight rim, which now for the first time make their appearance. The dating of this series would seem to be from about 1375 to the end of the century.[1]

An entirely new series of problems are presented by the vases, bottles, ewers and jars, since variation in shape and surface offer the decorators new opportunities to display their ingenuity and skill. For instance, vases of the various kinds may be circular in horizontal section, or octagonal, or even multi-faceted, and each makes special and different demands on the decorator. There may be decoration flowing freely over the whole surface as in the Umezawa bottle vase (Plate 38A) or it may be disposed in panels of various shapes set out in horizontal bands, which may themselves be broken down into panels (Colour Plate B, Plates 38B, 39A and B). Occasionally combinations of the panelling and horizontal banding may be found (Plate 39B). Through all of these are found a great diversity of motifs, some of which occur on the plates and others that do not. As with the plates the real difficulty is to determine what preceded the David vases; the second half of the century is more easily mapped, though in broader

---

[1] It will be seen that a five-year gap has been allowed between Groups 3 and 4. The problem implied here is discussed in my paper in *Ars Orientalis*, IX, 1973, pp. 89–101.

groups than in the case of the plates. At all stages it is essential to recognize that several workshops are involved in the manufacture of a relatively wide range of shapes and styles of decoration.

The large *kuan* jar decorated with cutaway panels with applied reliefs, in the David Foundation, is an important candidate for the earliest stratum (Colour Plate B). The relationship between the technique of decoration on this jar and that which is shown on the Fonthill vase is obvious (Plate 7A). In addition the construction of this unusually large piece is somewhat primitive and it is very roughly finished. Noteworthy is the fact that it is not until the fourteenth century that really large pots are produced, so that the early large specimens may justifiably be expected to display imperfections both in the finishing of the structure and in the control of the firing. In this instance, indeed, the glazing is careless, being uneven in a number of places, and somewhat casual in its application on the inside. The firing certainly presented grave difficulties, for a break appeared in the base, 10 cm. long and about 13 mm. wide at the widest point. Evidently the makers set great store by the piece and in order not to waste it the gaping hole was plugged with wood and plaster, which remain even today. The decoration broken up into bands and panels reflects the influence of Near Eastern metalwork, while the relief decoration resembles that of Chinese silverwork of the type seen in the cast silver comb in the Kempe Collection.[1] The 'cloud collar' elements on the shoulder filled with chrysanthemum and pomegranate alternately are features that are to persist for some time to come. The arrangement of the flower sprays is somewhat uncertain, lacking the careful neatness of those on the shoulder of Mr. and Mrs. Frederick Mayer's *mei-p'ing*, which should be dated rather later, to coincide with the second and third group of foliate plates (Plate 42A). The dating of the David Foundation *kuan* to the first period of about 1330 to 1340 receives some additional support, apart from the Fonthill vase, in the style of the pomegranate spray in the panel on the left in the illustration, when this is compared with that of the massive carved Lung-ch'üan celadon vase dated 1327.[2] The resemblance in general treatment is close despite the difference in technique.

Other vessels which seem to belong to this first period up to about 1345 are the large *kuan* with cover from the Pao-ting find[3] the associated octagonal-faceted bottle ewer and vase (Plates 39A, B), and the multi-faceted bottle vase in a private collection in Japan. The

---

[1] Gyllensvärd, *Catalogue of gold and silver in the Carl Kempe Collection*, No. 143.

[2] Plate 58.

[3] *Wên-wu*, 1965, No. 2, pp. 17–18 and 22. Plates 1–3.

UNDERGLAZE BLUE, COPPER RED DECORATED WARES

Pao-ting *kuan* seems from its apparently more accomplished handling to be a little later than the David Foundation *kuan*. The use of a well-controlled classic scroll and an angled key-fret band suggest a greater experience and improved handling of the materials; moreover the petal panel band round the bottom includes a more complicated decorative element in the form of a stylized lotus in place of the simple curlicue so often associated with the incised and relief beaded white wares of the early part of the century. The two octagonal vessels from Pao-ting (Plates 39A, B) display certain primitive features and a hesitancy in the treatment of some of the details.[1] The features they have in common with each other and a number of other pieces to be attributed to the same period are the plantain leaves with the solid central vein and dark edge, the slightly cursive key-fret band, which is in the form of a series of detached counter-clockwise turns with the last stroke always to the left, the petal panels forming wide border above and below the central band of decoration edged by classic scrolls and diaper. On the ewer the inverted S-curved tie between the spout and the body emphasizes the relationship between the early blue and white and some of the transitional white wares in which these S-curves are used to perform the service of handles. Linking these two specimens to others of the period is the treatment of the surface inside the lip of the vase which is carefully painted. This is a feature to be found on other bottle vases, both octagonal and circular, the Clark bottle being one of the latter (Plate 25). It is found for instance on the multi-faceted vase (Plate 38B) on which the plantain leaf and key-fret elements are also found. The finest example to be related to these three is the Umezawa vase with a similarly painted treatment inside the lip, a cursive meander round the foot and the freely painted scene of men in landscape round the body (Plate 38A).

In the examples so far mentioned we have already the full range of the organization of the decorations in panels, horizontal bands and panelled bands. A series of basic formulae to be repeated throughout the century is therefore already established in the second quarter of the period. Like the decoration of the plates these schemes and details are subject to the same general rules, moving gradually towards tighter symmetry and greater control of the elements. By mid century, that is from about 1345 to 1355 or 1360, the boldness and strength found in the David vases is seen in a wide range of material which includes *mei-p'ing*, *kuan* and gourd vases.

In this period the faceted *mei-p'ing* and gourd vases are among the most striking vessels, with boldness and variety of handling that is at least as fine as anything found among the plates of the same period.

---

[1] *Wên-wu*, 1965, No. 2, Plates 2–3.

The most remarkable of the faceted *mei-p'ing* is the one with cover that was discovered at Pao-ting in 1964 (Plate 40). On this the more usual treatment of lappets and bracketed medallions such as is found on the Mayer *mei-p'ing* (Plate 42A) is absent, the lappet or 'cloud collar' elements being retained as implied borders top and bottom, and the whole of the central area being used with great daring and freedom. The dragons are incised into the surface and reserved in white, except for a few details, against a tempestuous wave background of quite a different kind from that found on the David vases. On the top of the shoulder is a band of diamond diaper, which suggests a close relationship with the plates of the mid-century groups when this motif seems to have been introduced. The same motif occurs on the Victoria and Albert Museum *mei-p'ing*, a vase of a very different character, dated by Dr. Kikutaro Saito to the period 1340–49.[1] It is seen again on the mouth of the large jar in the Fitzwilliam Museum (Plate 42B), which is a curious mixture in form between a *mei-p'ing* and a *kuan*. This is a particularly unusual specimen because instead of the normal arrangement of four lappets and collar, there are six elements, the main field also being ornamented with six bracketed medallions all reserved against a knobbed scroll ground. Each panel and medallion, except the lappets on the shoulder, has a different decoration, the shoulder lappets having a tightly controlled wave pattern that is nearer to the David vase type than that of the Pao-ting vase. The wave pattern of the Pao-ting vase is more closely related to the octagonal gourd vase, from a Japanese collection, where this decoration forms a dividing band between the upper and lower bulb (Plate 41). Round the mouth of this vase there is once more the diamond diaper. The panels, both pictorial ones and the petal panels, are bordered by the curious ornamental split palmette deriving from the *lāmalif*, a feature seen in a slightly more primitive form on the Fitzwilliam jar and in an incipient stage on the band of panels on the Pao-ting ewer.[2] This is a motif very rarely seen on the plates and then only on the bracket foliate type in its most advanced form, the most magnificent specimen being the moulded Hobart plate in the Fogg Museum of Art and the reserve painted one in Ardebil (Plate 29A).

In the mid-century group, for which the way is opened by the Pao-ting *mei-p'ing*, the Fitzwilliam jar and the gourd vase reveal certain characteristics common in dishes from an early stage, for the first time. These are the hatched peony leaf (Plates 44A, 46), the open

---

[1] Kikutaro Saito, *Gendai no sometsuke ko* ('Yüan blue and white'), *Kobijutsu*, 18, 1967, pp. 25–41. In Japanese with an English summary.

[2] For a discussion on this type of panel see my paper 'Chinese ceramics and Islamic design', *PDF Colloquy* No. 3.

and the closed peony flower, the 'split' peony (Plate 43A)[1] and the David vase type wave band. The appearance of these elements coincides with a more carefully calculated organization of the decoration, together with the introduction of the shaded scaled animal or dragon and two entirely new forms.

One form is the taller type of *kuan* jar with long sloping shoulders, narrow neck flanged at the mouth and with two animal mask mounts for ring handles at the sides (Plate 45B). This from now on was to be popular, starting with rather a broad band of decoration round the body. The older smaller form continues parallel for some time but the decoration is invariably of the free kind that is unconfined by petal panels and usually has a wave band round the short neck as represented by the former Russell Collection one now in the British Museum (Plate 44A). The best examples of the type are the freely decorated ones which normally have boldly painted wave pattern of the David vase type encircling the short straight neck. A unique example is the one in the Fitzwilliam Museum in Cambridge (Colour Plate C) with ducks swimming among lotus, the leaves of some of the plants being painted as though drooping and weary, showing signs of decay. The last feature is peculiar and the example is the only one known in which something resembling a sponge has been used to apply the cobalt blue to the raw body, a technique known and quite commonly used in late seventeenth- and early eighteenth-century blue and white in Europe, yet is quite unparalleled in China at any other time. This is approximately the same date as that from Ardebil, a piece having hatched peony leaves and the David vase wave pattern. One peculiar feature of the painting of these vessels other than dishes, is the hatching of the peony leaves, and sometimes vine leaves. This hatched effect on a blue painted area is achieved by lightly scoring the surface before painting, then painting in the scored lines, which have been executed using a comb-like instrument, and thereafter carrying out the painting of the decoration in the ordinary way. Why this complicated method of decorating should have been decided upon is a complete mystery; it is of no help in the establishment of a chronological succession.

The other new form is the flattened rectangular flask with double lugs, usually in the form of dragons, on the shoulder (Plates 43A and B, 44B). The earliest example of this rare group is the one in the Garner Collection, which has a powerfully conceived and drawn dragon, with shaded scales, leaping from waves on each side. The wave pattern, related to the David vase type, is unusual on account of the triple plume kicking back against the main flow of the design, a

[1] *Ardebil*, Plate 27.

peculiarity first noted in the plate from Ardebil (Plate 28B) with herons in a pond. The rock forms on this flask are of an interesting spiky variety which occur again on the slightly later Ardebil flask (Plate 43A) in a milder handling. It seems possible that the Garner flask may be datable on account of the wave pattern to within five years before the David vases, if the wave pattern in this form is as early, but that the Ardebil flask is later, somewhat after the David vases, partly on account of the milder handling of the spiky rocks, from which the hatched leaf peonies grow up round the peacocks, whose plumage is treated in a linear style. The more ornamental treatment at the top of the side panels seems also to suggest a slightly later date. The other side of the flask (Plate 43B) is also interesting because of the lotus spray, which includes forms of that flower only occurring in the period up to about 1360. One is the triple spike flower, seen left and right of the lion, another is the flower in the centre between the bird and the beast. These flowers also occur on some of the plates of the same period, that is of Group 3 of the foliate type and Group 1 of the straight rimmed type. Both flowers can be seen on the moulded plate from Istanbul in Plate 30. In the painted form they have been modified slightly to suit the different technique. After 1360 in the later straight rimmed type, the fully opened flower does not occur at all, and the spiked centre type is somewhat changed. On a contemporary *mei-p'ing* in the Garner Collection the triple spiked flower appears in the scroll round the shoulder (Plate 46) and next to it, as though farther up the stem, an opening flower occurs with the stamens showing. This succession is repeated on the Ardebil flask. The leaves on both specimens are also similar; though some of the Garner ones are spiked, others have a curious twisted or coiled appearance. Clearly these two pieces are close in date, very soon after the middle of the century.

The spiky rock continues to appear on a number of examples of the immediate post-David vase period up to about 1360, and even afterwards in a very few cases. It is found on a large bowl decorated rather freely round the outside with the Three Friends in a wide band, with classic scroll and petal panels below (Plates 47A, B). Inside is an unusual variant of the lotus pond decoration with ducks. The scene is given additional interest by shifting the centre of the pattern to the right, forcing the artist to squeeze the right side of the scene into a more restricted space, while the left side, almost entirely omitted, is replaced by some more spiky rocks and a plantain shrub beside a balustraded terrace. The plantain leaves are unbroken and similar to those that sometimes occur on the straight rimmed plates of Groups 1 and 2 (Plates 34B, 35A). The spiky rock and the coiled lotus leaves are seen again on the octagonal gourd vase in Topkapu Seray (Plate 48), a rather mechanically handled example displaying a very carefully calculated approach to the treatment of surface as well as a meticulous slightly stiff execution. The pattern book was probably studied with diligence and then adhered to rigidly.

This rather large and varied group leads on into the next stage which can best be aligned with the later stages of Group 2 and the whole of Group 3 of the straight rimmed plates. The boundaries, however, are hard to define with precision. In this third series of vessels the hatched leaf virtually disappears, only one specimen can perhaps be included, and this is a *mei-p'ing* in a Japanese collection,[1] in which the form has changed abruptly and uncharacteristically to a rather square shouldered type, with the peony scroll standing out in an isolated manner against broad areas of white. The neck too has changed to a shorter form with a flatter mouth rim, similar to that on a *mei-p'ing* which has a boldly, well-spaced peony scroll round the body, with a 'cloud collar' above and a very precisely drawn classic scroll below (Plate 49). The flower sprays in the collar have undergone a change; the peony, pomegranate and chrysanthemum remain, but the fourth is a five-petalled flower with a straight edged leaf in place of the expected camellia, and in each case small curls and spikes have been added as fillers, producing an effect of slight fussiness in this area. The main scroll and the petal panels below are executed with great care, the outlines of the stems, the leaves and panels show up clearly against a slightly paler wash filling, a peculiarity of treatment to be seen repeated in the Boston *kuan* with lion-headed reliefs at the sides (Plate 45A). A change of style is clearly indicated in this jar, which is less freely and strongly treated than earlier examples of the form. In place of the earlier wide band round the body with a narrower one on the shoulder the scheme has now been organized in three bands, which has resulted in the main band diminishing in width and in the upper one widening considerably to accommodate the large lappets. As with the *mei-p'ing*, the main decorative band, this time with a dragon and clouds, and the lotus panels are outlined and then filled with a paler wash. The heavy, large scale classic scroll is similarly treated. The flower sprays in the large lappets have the stems executed in a stringy as well as fussy manner not unlike that of the *mei-p'ing*.

Parallel with this outline and wash manner of painting combined with a thin linear technique is the older style without obvious outlines, the whole decoration being carried out in about the same concentration of blue. It is however apparent that the breaking of the surface into

[1] *Sekai Tōji Zenshū*, Vol. 11, Plate 29.

narrower decorative bands has been adopted in this style as well. A fine example of this late stage, after the elimination of the hatched leaves and the introduction of the narrow bands, is the *kuan* in the Cleveland Museum of Art (Plate 45B). The calculations upon which the design is based are extremely nice, the lappets of which there are six, exactly matching the peonies in the lower band. The alternation of the flowers in the lappets and the upward and downward movement of the birds, two down-flying birds facing two upturned peonies, is a charmingly executed conception. The lotus scroll in the upper band on the shoulder is also worked out very carefully so that each flower is isolated sufficiently from the leaves to stand out clearly against the white ground. The stem of the scroll is of the thin spindly variety with a few filler spikes added, and the leaves themselves are uniformly of the twisted or coiled variety that was beginning to appear in the earlier series that included the Ardebil flask (Plates 43A, B). The rather crowded arrangement of the lappets is in marked contrast to the well-spaced, carefully organized decoration of the rest of the surface and is instantly noticeable. Other examples of a similar treat-ment of a rather mechanical filling of lappets, and the breaking of the surface into a greater number of decorative bands, are fairly numerous, and the tendency towards this proliferation of bands marks the end of a particular line of development and opens the way through its very complexity to a revolution, or revision, to a simpler organization. The increasing symmetry, numerically and in the elements used as well as in the copy-book accuracy are all indications of a fully matured style, and in the next and final stage from about 1370 to the end of the century a similar pattern to that already encountered in the last group of dishes must be expected.

The last stage from about 1370 onwards is exemplified by many pieces in both blue and white and in copper red. Because of this it is possible to turn directly from the Cleveland *kuan* in blue and white to a bottle vase in copper red in which the elements of the final style are displayed (Plate 50A). There is still the urge on the part of the designers to break up the surface into a series of bands made up of unrelated elements, but there is now a change in the proportions; the main band, which had been shrinking, is suddenly enlarged and once more plays an important role. The lappet band is reduced to a narrow ornamental framing band somewhat resembling a pelmet, and the upper area is split into a number of much smaller bands. The main peony scroll is carried out in the same carefully calculated manner as on the Cleveland jar, and in style there is relatively little difference between the two. There are, however, certain elements identifying the late style and which introduce features that lead on naturally into

the fifteenth-century Ming style. First the key-fret border at the foot
and at the neck. In earlier examples, including the Cleveland jar, this
consists of detached elements, often slightly angled, and from the
innermost point unwinds, so to speak, in counter-clockwise direction,
each fret standing on its own. Now the treatment is quite different,
though the general impression remains unchanged. The frets are
paired in a tight S-formation and are to continue in this form into the
fifteenth century when it can be found on a series of dishes of characteristic early Ming style in Ardebil[1]. The petal panels also undergo an
apparently unimportant change. These are no longer detached one
from the next as in the earlier pieces, but are run together in a continuous band. Here again is a treatment that carries straight through
to the fifteenth-century style. The only exception to this handling is
to be found on the copper red ewers (Plate 50B). The lappets, reduced
to an ornamental border, have lost the floral, bird and other decorative
filling and are either simply striated as in this instance of the ewer, or
they are filled with a flat wash of colour. The latter course is generally
preferred when a rather smaller size is chosen, as on the cut-down
bottle (Plate 51A), and in this form they continue into the middle of
the fifteenth century.[2] The plantain leaves rising stiffly above the key-
fret band are different again from the earlier type in which the central
vein was painted in a solid line; now it is open, being delineated so
that it stands out white against the striated leaf. This also leads on into
the fifteenth century, and it can be found on many pieces up to and
including the Hung-chih temple vase dated to 1496.[3] A final point to
notice is the introduction of the fungus scroll, which, it will be
recalled, suddenly appeared on the dishes in this last period. These
basic motifs and their manner of treatment unify the whole group of
blue and white and copper red in the last thirty years of the fourteenth
century. In addition it is characteristic of the pieces of this period that
they are all heavy, thick walled and strongly made. Many of the
vessels are of very large size, and there is also a largeness of scale in all
the decoration.

The cut-down vase (Plate 51A) introduces into the heavy wide-
based form a decorative element already seen in the plates. This is the
free disposal of the flowers of the four seasons, one of which it will be
noticed is here growing from a rather debased spiky rock. A similar
treatment can be seen on the rather stiffly painted, but very attractive,

[1] *Ardebil*, Plate 30.
[2] See the blue and white leys jar in the David Foundation, No. B685, a specimen
of the stepped base group associated with the so-called Interregnum. It is here a
shoulder band.
[3] Percival David Foundation, No. 680.

blue and white example in Philadelphia (Plate 51B). The same rather free treatment is seen also on the bowls (Plates 52A, B) and is particularly striking in the one in Istanbul, which is illustrated by Addis.[1] This massive basin or bowl is interesting on account of the floret-like element appearing in the petal panels round the base, a motif also seen on the massive twelve-lobed *kuan* type jars (Plate 53) of which examples are found in Japan, the British Museum and the Baur Foundation in Geneva. In these the flowers of the twelve months grow up each lobe from the familiar spiky rock. The painting is strong and the decoration of each panel is admirably spaced; unfortunately not all examples are equally well fired, a fact for which their great size may well account.

Bottle vases, ewers, bowls and basins are among the most common forms in this group; the *mei-p'ing*, however, is rare. Indeed at the moment we can only record one survivor (Plate 54), painted in copper red, which was recovered from a tomb on the outskirts of Nanking. This splendid piece is a link not only with the earlier fourteenth-century style but also with that of the fifteenth century. The division of the surface recalls the high style of the mid fourteenth century, but the treatment of the individual elements differs and the introduction of small overlapping lappets at the base of the neck looks forward into the early fifteenth-century style.[2] Particularly striking is the absence of the conventional narrow band of decoration, be it a classic scroll or a diaper band, between the freely painted landscape scene and the chrysanthemum scroll band on the shoulder. The wave pattern, too, has been introduced in a very curious position between the continuous petal panel band and the main field. The treatment of the plantain leaves with the open central vein should particularly be noticed.

To the same family of the late fourteenth century belong the small plates and cup-stands (Plates 55A, B). On the backs of both types are petal panels based on the foot-ring. The blue and white plate (Plate 55A) decorated with a peony spray in the central medallion with a very neatly organized six-flowered lotus scroll surrounding it and with a key-fret pattern on the rim, is typical of the class. It should be noticed that the very shallow well remains free of decoration; this is characteristic of the plates. The cup-stands on the other hand are lobed with eight bracket-lobes which extend from the rim down to the foot-ring. These are clearly made using twin moulds. As with the plates the centre is adorned with a floral spray; in the one illustrated

---

[1] 'A group of underglaze red: a postscript', *T.O.C.S.*, 36, 1964–66, pp. 89–102, Plate 83b.

[2] Addis, op. cit., p. 101. The drawing shows the plantain leaves and overlapping lappets very clearly.

C. *Wine jar in blue and white. Ht. 30·3 cm.*
Fitzwilliam Museum

D. *Plate, white dragon on blue ground. Diam.* 15·9 *cm.*
Percival David Foundation

UNDERGLAZE BLUE, COPPER RED DECORATED WARES

in Plate 55B, this is a peony, but the lotus also occurs. Unlike the plates on which the floral medallion is encircled by simple painted rings, the cup-stands have a shaped ring of clay sprigged on and usually painted with a small petal motif. Round this is again a floral scroll of six flowers and this is sometimes slightly cramped into a more restricted area than is the case with the plates. The well, as the form seems to demand, is decorated with floral sprays, in this instance lotus, while flattened rim is filled with a classic scroll, an invariable feature. Some examples of cup-stands are flanged at the rim. The examples with the flanged rim are generally the smaller of the two types, being about 19 cm. in diameter, as against 20 cm. diameter of the type without the flange. The sizes of these two variants of the same shape continue into the fifteenth century, though by that time the central flanged ring characteristic of the cup-stand form has been eliminated. As the ring was probably sprig moulded and thus stuck directly on to the body, it would be quite simple to get rid of and the trouble of making a new mould for the dish would be avoided.[1]

Among other types to be attributed to this final stage in the four-teenth-century style are a number of copper red painted *kendi*. One of these in the Dreyfus Collection is an obvious candidate (Plate 56A), but the Garner one appears later,[2] the leaves of the peony having completely changed into something more nearly resembling the type seen on a number of early fifteenth-century bowls of which the David Foundation one, No. A611, is representative.[3]

Finally, before leaving the subject of blue and white, one distinctive class remains to be discussed. This is the 'white slip reserve' class, so named by Ayers, who describes some of them.[4] The dating of this class might present great difficulties were it not for the existence of two bracket-foliated plates, one in Teheran and the other in Topkapu Seray. These two have fourteen foliations and thus would in accord-ance with the scheme set out here be attributed to the second, trans-itional group between the wholly eccentric early series and the fully developed third group of mid fourteenth-century date. The decorative motifs in white of dragons, phoenixes, kylin, and lotus and chrysan-themum sprays are intimately related to those used in other material

---

[1] That the ring was sprigged is suggested by the fact that a Lung-ch'üan celadon example, recently presented to the British Museum, had had the ring added in this way. The piece was broken straight across the middle and the glaze had seeped under the edge of the ring, proof of this method of construction. There seems good reason to believe the same method was used in the other examples.

[2] 'The Arts of the Ming Dynasty', O.C.S., 1957, No. 153.

[3] Percival David Foundation, *Illustrated Catalogue*, Section 3, Plate VIII.

[4] J. Ayers, 'Some Characteristic Wares of the Yüan Dynasty', T.O.C.S., 29, 1954–55, pp. 69–83.

attributed to the period between about 1340 and 1355. The number of pieces that survive is limited at present to these two dishes, three small plates each with dragons and flaming pearls (Colour Plate D), the Musée Guimet's *mei-p'ing* with a dragon almost identical to that on the Teheran dish and the spouted bowl in the Victoria and Albert Museum (Plates 57A, B). The existence of this spouted bowl is another indication of a relatively early date, as the blue and white, and the copper red painted examples together with the plain blue one from Pao-ting with gilt decoration (Plate 54B), and the Malcolm Collection Shu-fu type one, formerly gilt, all belong to a group that was probably not made after about the middle of the century. With the exception of the unusually delicately made Malcolm example, these are all rather stoutly constructed and are unglazed on the rim, a feature which may be accepted as early.

4

LUNG-CH'ÜAN CELADONS

An examination of the celadons of Chekiang and the classification and dating of these stonewares and porcellanous wares must be a daunting one for any student of Chinese ceramics. Even when the subject is attacked by a specialist in the field the results have been inconclusive and to some extent confusing. The establishment of anything resembling a coherent chronological pattern for the Yüan dynasty, a bare ninety years, presents even greater difficulties. The manifold problems of the period are so closely tied to preconceived notions based on imperfect definitions, that one may perhaps be pardoned for a reluctance to attempt a detailed examination of the products of Chekiang. It seems quite foolhardy to contemplate the possibility of establishing a chronology for such a brief period of time and for such a notoriously difficult group of wares in view of the scarcity of archaeological evidence. The reasons even apart from these are not far to seek. From Hangchou at the northern end of Chekiang to the southernmost extremity of the province the area is a source of raw materials, which are so closely related chemically and physically, owing to their common origin in geological time, that the same basic types were inevitably produced in almost every group of kilns. The variations are mainly those of the techniques employed not only in the construction and form of the vessels, but also in decoration, yet even with these differences it is hard to distinguish pieces from different districts or even individual kilns. The fact that Kuan type wares produced at the famous Chiao-t'an, or Temple of Heaven, kiln are admitted by even so experienced a specialist as Dr. Ch'ên Wan-li to be virtually indistinguishable from the contemporary copies made in the Lung-ch'üan valley must make us wary from the outset.[1] Whether at a later date microscopic, chemical or other tests will help clarify a confused situation remains and is likely to remain an open question for some

[1] Ch'ên Wan-li, *Chung-kuo ch'ing-tz'ŭ shih-lüeh* ('Outline history of Chinese celadon'), Peking, 1956, p. 28.

63

time to come. About fifteen years ago Gompertz drew attention to some of the difficulties which face us here, when he surveyed the whole evolution of Chinese celadon, and he pointed out that not only were 'the Lung-ch'üan and other celadon kilns in southern Chekiang . . . in no sense official factories', but, and this is an important point, that 'they were unaffected by the change of dynasty'.[1] These facts together with the reality of an expanding export trade deliberately stimulated first by the Sung for essential economic reasons, and subsequently exploited by the Mongols for purely selfish ones, tends further to confuse a picture already generally admitted to be complicated. There seems to be no clear lead into this picture which would distinguish the parts and help to isolate the essential components so that a clearly defined pattern could be discerned. The best that can be attempted is to use as a basis the largeness of scale and sturdiness of construction that characterizes the greater part of Yüan production and see whether this yields anything of interest. Partly because of this and partly because every student has his own method of approach to any particular problem, there is one point which it is important to make clear at this stage. The use of such terms as *kinuta*, Tenryūji and Shichiji as descriptive notions of colour will be eschewed. The use of these rather popular terms is hazardous since they depend so much on subjective judgement; moreover glaze colour and texture, to which within limits they refer, are so largely dependent on the preparation of the batch of material, the chances of firing and the placement in the kiln, that it is rash to tie down particular colours and textures to specific periods.

When we turn to the wares themselves, we find that while Gompertz is perfectly correct in emphasizing that the kilns were unaffected by the change of dynasty so far as the more commonly produced and used vessels were concerned, changes would seem in fact already to have begun in the thirteenth century in some of the less common vessels, such as large dishes and plates, evidently produced for the export market, or for the foreign merchants resident at the major ports, where there had long been semi-independent groups of foreigners. It has to be remembered, too, that the Lung-ch'üan region, and that slightly to the south, where other groups of kilns were producing similar material, were very well placed to supply the trade through Wên-chou and Ch'üan-chou, which during the last half-century of Sung and throughout the Yüan carried the heaviest trade of any of the Chinese ports.

It is significant in this connection that as a result of cross-fertilization between Lung-ch'üan and Jao-chou, certain forms in one area

[1] G. St. G. M. Gompertz, *Chinese Celadon Wares*, London, 1958, p. 61.

antedate those in the other. Much has been accomplished in studies along these lines since the publication of Pope's views expressed in *Chinese Porcelains from the Ardebil Shrine*.[1] It now seems that large plates with flattened rims, initially straight at the edge, made their first appearance at Lung-ch'üan. When the basic form was taken up in the blue and white in Jao-chou, it was the more novel type with bracket lobing that was introduced, and that continued to be used there in this ware for a large part of the period covered by the early industrialization and development of porcelain in the region. As this form with the flattened rim can be clearly traced to a Near Eastern, or even East European, metal form,[2] and Lung-ch'üan was better placed than Jao-chou to receive it in the initial stages of the expansion of the foreign market, this primacy in the production of dishes comes as no surprise. The mass production of these plates, probably from the date of their first appearance in Lung-ch'üan, makes it almost impossible to distinguish late Sung examples from those of the earlier years of the Yüan, except perhaps by the restraint in the decoration in the former. To this we must add the known existence of something like one hundred and fifty kilns datable to the Yüan, about half of them in the vicinity of Ta-yao and Chi-k'ou.[3] Thus any hope of definitive dating without inscribed or otherwise documented pieces vanishes. The only securely dated Lung-ch'üan celadon, and this from Ta-yao, remains the massive trumpet-mouthed vase with robust baluster body in the David Foundation (Plate 58). The inscription on this magnificent vessel with its bounding contours, runs round the inner edge of the lip and includes a date corresponding to 1327.[4] Even apart from this date the vessel includes elements that well qualify it for a Yüan attribution. It has all the weight, strength and boldness combined

[1] J. Pope, op. cit., p. 153, et seq.

[2] A. Pope, *Survey of Persian Art*, Vol. VI, Plate 1315B and Smirnov, *Argenterie Orientale*, Plate 101. See also M. Medley, *Metalwork and Chinese ceramics*, Plates 11a, b.

[3] Chin Tsu-ming, 'Lung-ch'üan Chi-k'ou ch'ing-tz'ŭ yao-chih t'iao-ch'a chi-lüeh' ('Short report on the celadon kiln sites at Chi-k'ou in Lung ch'üan'), *K'ao-ku*, 1962, No. 10, pp. 535-8; and Chu Po-ch'ien, 'Report on the excavation of celadon kiln sites in Lung-ch'üan in Chekiang Province', *Wên-wu*, 1963, No. 1, pp. 27-35.

[4] The inscription has been translated: 'Chang Chin-ch'êng of the hamlet of Wan-an by the Liu (-hua) Hill at Chien-ch'üan in Kua-ts'ang, a humble believer in the Three Precious Ones (i.e. Buddhism) has baked a pair of large flower vases to be placed for evermore before the Buddha in the great hall of Chüeh-lin Temple, with the prayer that the blessing of peace, happiness and prosperity may attend his family. Carefully written on a lucky day in the second autumn month of the cyclical year *ting-mao*, the fourth year of the period T'ai-ting.' For the identification of Wan-an with Ta-yao, see Gompertz, *Chinese Celadon Wares*, p. 61, following *Che-chiang T'ung-chih*, 1899, Ch. 21, f. 22b et seq. See also *Ceramic Art of China*, No. 115, 1972, Plates 78-9 for details of the inscription.

with passages of elaborate workmanship that are the hallmarks of the period. There is another feature, that could not be noticed by Ayers in his study of Yüan types, though he does so in connection with a vase in the Baur Collection: this is the peculiar treatment of the base.[1] It is cut right away through the bottom just inside the foot-ring, the hole being sealed from the inside by laying a saucer upside down over the aperture, where it is held in place solely by the fired glaze. It must have been placed there before the upper part of the body and the neck were luted on. This fantastic method of construction is a common feature of really large vases and wine jars, and may occasionally be found on large basins and bulb bowls; very rarely it may occur on dishes. The division of the surface into a series of formal and natural-istic bands of decoration is a formula already familiar in both the white wares and the blue and white. It is noticeable, too, that there is a relationship between the handling of the floral scrolls on this vase and some of those that appear on the shoulder of the cobalt blue and copper red decorated jar, which we assign to about 1330, in the earliest stratum of the blue and white.[2] Also worthy of remark is that the shape of the vase, with its wide trumpet mouth, is peculiar to the Lung-ch'üan repertory of form, and is the only one virtually unrepre-sented in any other ware in China in this period. It seems, however, to have become a popular shape at Lung-ch'üan and has many smaller variants, some carved, some with sprig-moulded decoration and some with ferruginous brown spots of the type known to the Japanese as *tobi-seiji* (Plates 59A, B).

In taking this one dated vase as a starting point from which to attempt a chronological grouping, we are immediately faced with complications resembling those already encountered in connection with our treatment of blue and white, for which we had to depend on the David vases. Although in this case we know something about the antecedents, the position is made less simple than one might expect by the existence not only of the large number of kilns active at the time and distributed over a wide area, but also by the multiplicity of forms as well as a degree of specialization with regard to techniques.

In the last forty years of the thirteenth century and the first thirty years of the fourteenth century, there must have been a formidable quantity of material produced, in much of which one would expect to find indications of the evolution towards a mid-Yüan type. This is indeed the case, but only so far as those types that are most easily identified on account of their size and shape are concerned. It is not

[1] J. Ayers, *The Baur Collection: Chinese ceramics*, Vol. 1, No. A109, Geneva, 1968.
[2] See Colour Plate B.

easy, for instance, when one turns to the smaller more ordinary bowls and saucers, which were part of the common production for domestic use in every household, to determine the line of development, because for purely practical economic reasons the kilns would naturally continue making the same well-tried shapes over a long period with little discernible variation. Yet if one looks 'at these popular wares rather closely there is something to be gained, since the characteristic solidity and the robustness of contour may be observed even in many of the more common products of the large number of kilns. Apart from glaze variations, such as are inevitable in reduction firing, it is possible to identify a great number of saucers of rather heavy construction. These have a thick foot-ring, usually glazed over, with part of the base, if not all of it, left unglazed. This seems to have been a common Yüan practice, and one that applies to a wide range of shapes. Many of the bowls and saucers bear an impressed mark, either of seal characters or of a floral element, in the centre. Among the most common seal marks is that of *Ho-pin i-fan*,[1] which probably came into use in the latter part of the Southern Sung period and continued through perhaps as far as the second or third decade of the fourteenth century. Later examples of this type (Plate 60A) may often be lobed at the rim and have a thin line of white slip trailed from the notch at the rim towards the centre, emphasizing the lobing and dividing the surface into a series, usually of five or six compartments round the inner wall. This feature itself is one of a number of characteristic changes that occurred in the use of surface in the Yüan period.

Another form in which we can see the transition from Sung to Yüan is the small multi-lobed cup with rounded walls and straight rim. These are found in both Lung-ch'üan and Kuan, but whether they started in Kuan and were passed on to Lung-ch'üan and made in imitation of Kuan, or were initiated in Lung-ch'üan, it is not possible to discover. They were probably first made during the thirteenth century and continued into early Yüan, gradually becoming thicker and heavier in body; one or two examples even display debased bracket lobing of the wall, a feature particularly of those which seem to be late in date. The shape is a common one in contemporary silver, as may be remarked in such a fourteenth-century cup as that shown by the Nelson Gallery of Art at the exhibition of 'Chinese Art under the Mongols'.[2] In silver this characteristic form often includes a repoussé five- or six-petalled flower in the bottom, a feature sometimes

---

[1] *Ho-pin i-fan*, 'Pattern bequeathed on the bank of the river', an obscure reference to an emperor of legendary times.
[2] Cleveland Museum of Art, 1968, No. 33a.

imitated in the white porcelain of Jao-chou,[1] but not very commonly seen in the celadons.

The influence of metalwork, exceptionally strong in the Mongol period, was not only that of the native tradition. Near Eastern metalwork also made a strong impact, and this may be seen in the unusual bowls, small at the foot, with a generous outward curving wall turned neatly inwards at the top to a well-controlled mouth rim. The carved and incised decoration generally found on these bowls is held very much in restraint, and is subdued to the form like an echo of the elegant refinement of the Sung, when it is likely that the form was first introduced (Plate 60B). On the inside of the vessel the decoration may take the form of an abbreviated floral scroll which is nearly an abstract design, sometimes indeed reaching this extreme. On the outside the simple lotus petal carving emphasizes the more austere and refined attitude of the Chinese when faced with this alien form as compared with its elaborate, often extravagant treatment in Islamic hands.[2] It is no surprise to find that this type of bowl appears first in the Chekiang celadons, since the area was more immediately open to outside influences, such as those from the Islamic world, than were places like Jao-chou so much farther inland and more remote from the ports. It was only later, in the blue and white, when Jao-chou became predominant, that this form was found in Kiangsi. The type continued there intermittently into the fifteenth century, changing very little from its original thirteenth-century pattern, when it was introduced perhaps primarily for the foreign market, although the relatively large numbers of small examples, about 10 cm. in diameter in celadon, also suggest a native interest in this shape.

Another vessel based on a metal prototype was the spouted bowl, which had its origins in silver in the late twelfth or early thirteenth century probably in the region of central Asia where it adjoins the Persian frontier. We already know this form in the underglaze blue decorated pieces from the Jao-chou region, as well as others in copper red and in *ch'ing-pai*. The Lung-ch'üan examples, however, are very much heavier and more solid in construction, and they lack the curl of clay under the rising spout, which in Jao-chou was added in slavish imitation of the silver originals, as shown in the ones from the hoard unearthed in Anhui and dating from 1333.[3] The Lung-ch'üan type is rarely decorated, the charm of the pieces being largely dependent

---

[1] Cleveland Catalogue, No. 110.

[2] A. Lane, *Early Islamic Pottery*, Plate 89a.

[3] *Ko-shao An-hui Ho-fei fa-hsien ti Yüan-tai chin-yin ch'i-p'an* ('Yüan dynasty gold and silver vessels discovered at Ho-fei in An-hui'), *Wên-wu*, 1957, No. 2, pp. 51–8; and M. Medley, *Metalwork and Chinese ceramics*, Plate 14a.

upon the thickness, colour and quality of the glaze, though one is recorded in a Japanese collection with carved petal panels round the outside.[1] Such other pieces as are decorated are of *tobi-seiji*, or spotted celadon, variety, with the dark brown ferruginous spots as carefully disposed as they are on the vases and plates. Rarest of all of this spotted type are those represented by the one in the Tōhata Collection in Japan, with copper red spots, the effect of which is very striking. The glaze of this piece is of exceptional quality, and unlike the Jao-chou pieces of this shape, which have an unglazed base, it has the glaze running over the foot and over most of the base; there is only a narrow unglazed band, which shows the scar of a firing stand. Another one of about half the size of this is in the Fujita Collection.

The more common and purely Chinese shapes, especially of bowls, often with simple carved lotus petal decoration round the outside and either straight or slightly everted at the rim, remained common currency for both domestic and overseas markets for a long period. Many have been found abroad, having been recovered from sites in the Philippines, south-east Asia and the whole Indonesian archipelago, as well as from sites in the Near East such as Fostat. Even farther afield a few have been recovered from East Africa, where they have been cemented into the walls of mosques and into the brickwork of tomb towers.[2] These cannot date earlier than the thirteenth century or later than the end of the fifteenth century, the dating and wide distribution of specimens of this type largely coinciding with the period of China's greatest maritime adventures. The later examples of the thirteenth and fourteenth centuries differ from the earlier Southern Sung ones in that the foot-ring is usually glazed over and the base left exposed to take the firing stand in the kiln. The coarse, more clumsy examples must have come from many of the less important kilns scattered throughout Chekiang and perhaps from among what would have been regarded as seconds or rejects by some of the major kilns such as Ta-yao and Chi-k'ou to the south of Lung-ch'üan itself. The poor colour and rough finish of many pieces lend support to this view, but some of the others were probably inferior lines produced at such kilns as those around Wên-chou, in imitation of the esteemed Lung-ch'üan type, but intended primarily for local use.

One small saucer shape which attained some popularity during the period was a shallow type with low outward flaring sides, and a sharp reversal of the curvature and contraction to the low thick foot-ring. These shapes, with a certain angularity of profile, are not uncommon

[1] Fujita Sale Catalogue, Osaka, 1929, Lot No. 303.
[2] James Kirkman, 'The great pillars of Malindi', *Oriental Art*, 2, 1958, p. 58.

in the Lung-chüan repertory and are associated not only with round saucers and stem-cups, but also with hexagonal and octagonal ones; there are even a few square ones (Plate 68A). The saucers generally have an impressed character in the centre, or a flower-like element (Plate 61A), but the more angular forms generally have more complicated decoration included in the moulds from which they have been pressed out (Plates 66, 67B).

Moulding techniques, both of vessels and decorations, were much exploited in the celadons during the Mongol period and played an important part in the creation of a distinctive Yüan style in the region. One of the characteristic techniques of Yüan especially associated with the Lung-ch'üan kilns is the use of sprig-moulding. This consists of decorative motifs, formed in small open moulds, being applied directly to the surface of a vessel generally while it is still in a comparatively soft state. The technique was first used in Yüeh wares as early as the third century but was not extensively employed until the T'ang dynasty for the decoration of earthenware tomb figures and vessels.[1] After this period the practice seems to have been abandoned and was only re-introduced, at least in the aristocratic wares of the Southern Sung, some time in the thirteenth century shortly before the collapse of the dynasty. It occurs not only in the Lung-ch'üan celadons, but also in some of the Chün, which are discussed in the next chapter. In some respects the technique was an easier and cheaper method of decoration than carving and incising, which demanded a sensitive control of the cutting tool. It was thus better suited to the mass-production techniques which became increasingly widespread during the thirteenth and fourteenth centuries in response to the expanding demand. In view of the long lapse of time between the sprig moulding of T'ang and its later re-appearance in late Sung, it seems to have been an independent development, but one which once again was inspired, as it had been in T'ang, by the elaborate decoration of metalwork. Its use in the Lung-ch'üan celadons is amply demonstrated in the earlier stages in the small plates with flattened rim, basically a metal form, in which two fish swim under a sea-green or bluish grey glaze (Plate 61B). These small pieces may have begun to appear about the middle of the thirteenth century, and it cannot have been long before other decorative motifs were added, but the range of motifs was still limited to such things as peony flowers and leaves linked by trailed slip stems. The latter decoration is found mainly on vases, like the *mei-p'ing* in the Seligman Collection (Plate 62A), or on incense burners, in the form of the Han period *lien* standing on three

[1] *Sekai tōji zenshū*, Vol. 8, Plate 119a for a Yüeh example and Vol. 9, Plates 49–50 for sixth- and seventh-century examples.

stumpy feet.[1] As time went by the decorations became more varied, complex and lavish, achieving in some cases an extravagance and splendour not found in other wares using this technique. The skill with which the potters handled these moulded reliefs gained for the wares so ornamented a prestige that put them into the highest and most aristocratic class of Yüan production from Lung-ch'üan.

Another and much more spectacular use of moulded decoration was subsequently evolved. Up to about the end of the thirteenth century and even perhaps later the practice of applying moulded elements directly to the surface before glazing continued to be found satisfactory, but the ingenuity of the potters could not be indefinitely restrained; it had to press on to a new mode of expression. As a result of the craftsman's urge to experiment a remarkable discovery was made that was peculiarly well suited from the aesthetic point of view to the celadon wares. Under certain conditions it was found possible to 'float' a moulded relief on the surface of the glaze. Thus instead of applying the relief directly to the unglazed body and later adding the glaze so that it covered the decoration, the potters now began to glaze the whole piece, whether plain or with previously carved decoration, and then to lay the moulded decorative elements on the surface of the unfired glaze. Here in the subsequent firing it remained to burn a brownish or rust colour untouched by glaze, producing a pleasing contrast in both colour and texture. One of the most handsome examples of this treatment is the large plate in the David Foundation (Colour Plate E), of which there are a number of other specimens with dragon, clouds, flaming pearl and florets. The underglaze application of precisely the same elements in the sprig-moulding technique and using the same basic arrangement of the elements may be seen in the massive rectangular flask also in the Foundation (Plate 63). As the large dish was almost certainly made for export, so too was the flask, a form wholly alien to the Chinese tradition; but there is one important feature, admirably demonstrated in these two specimens, to which attention must be drawn. It will be noticed that the plate, ornamented with unglazed reliefs, is an object which when placed in the kiln for firing will present the decoration in the horizontal plane, while the flask will present the same elements in the vertical plane. On the flask the decoration has been firmly fixed to the surface before glazing; had it been laid on the vertical surface over the glaze, an almost impossible achievement, the result in the firing would have been disastrous, since when the glaze melted, the reliefs would either have slipped or become distorted through their own weight when superimposed on a

[1] *Sekai tōji zenshū*, Vol. 10, Plate 46 from the Hakkutsuru Museum is a particularly good example.

medium which becomes relatively fluid at the high temperature required to fuse it to the body. This means that on surfaces that are to remain vertical in the kiln the 'floating' technique is impossible; 'floating' can only succeed if the object remains with the decoration in the horizontal position, so that neither slipping nor distortion can occur.

The practice of floating reliefs on the glaze, sometimes painting or washing them first with a colouring medium, became popular during the fourteenth century, and dishes, plates and saucers decorated in this way are fairly numerous. Many are simple plates and dishes with narrow flattened rim, often produced on the fast wheel using a template, the reliefs being applied after drying and glazing as described above. It was a quick and relatively easy method of production, lending itself to a wide variety of decoration, only limited by the imagination of the designer and the shape of the object, and it was perhaps regarded by the customer as an ornamental luxury; certainly the objects on which these relief designs are found can have had little practical purpose.

The repertory of decoration in this technique seems to have developed from the same series of motifs as those found in sprig moulding, the twin fish being especially popular in the initial stages, perhaps closely followed by the sinuous pairs of 'fleshy dragons' of various sizes. These are curious newt-like creatures, with curling, bifurcated tails, chasing each other in pairs round the centre of a plate (Plate 62B), a popular design also found on the Ting wares of the north as well as on the *ch'ing-pai* of Jao-chou. Gradually other motifs seem to have been added and the shape to which they were applied elaborated to include foliate rimmed plates and lobed saucers. A comparatively early example of a plate with hand-cut foliate rim is one with fruiting sprays shown in Plate 64A, with pomegranate, melon and peach, the fruits themselves in remarkably high relief, so high in fact as to make the piece completely non-functional. The bracket foliations numbering six and a half—a very strange number—would seem to imply an early date, as do the inconsistencies in cutting of the foliation themselves. Probably a little later in date, and mechanically produced using twin moulds, is the example with birds on peach branches in the David Foundation, an example with very pale buff reliefs against a grey-blue glaze (Plate 64B). Also to this mechanically produced series belongs the Brundage Collection plate with multi-scalloped rim and fluted well, decorated with a pair of phoenixes and butterflies disposed round a central chrysanthemum flower. This, in its way, is an ambitious example, the birds and the butterflies being slightly darker in colour and redder in tone than the central flower; the glaze is a pronounced grey-green. Among the lobed dishes the most attractive are those with rocks, a prunus tree and crescent moon in unglazed relief, with a delicately incised prunus spray under the glaze linking the different parts of the design, which is neatly disposed around the plain central field. On these the prunus flowers and buds are painted with a thick white pigment, and the rocks are generally coloured dark. The elements are very pleasingly treated with the crescent moon sometimes seeming to emerge from behind the prunus and sometimes floating free. The specimen showing the incised decoration best is that from the Eumorfopoulos Collection, now in the British Museum (Plate 65). All these plates and saucers are rather stoutly constructed and have a surprisingly small foot-ring and rather deeply recessed base, which is always glazed, the exposed foot-ring being burnt reddish brown. They all probably date from the middle and late years of the Mongol period. There are a few rather massive carved and incised pieces with small sparingly placed unglazed reliefs which may run into the Ming dynasty at the end of the fourteenth century, or possibly a little later, but these are no longer so attractive and are generally awkward in their overall proportions.

One of the most teasing problems which must have faced the Lung-ch'üan craftsmen, after the introduction of the technique of floating a relief on the glaze surface, was how a similar effect could be achieved on a surface that would be vertical or steeply inclined in the kiln. The solution, when found, turned out to be simple, ingenious and effective. It consisted quite simply of selecting those areas intended to stand out in unglazed contrast and painting them with wax or oil before applying the glaze to the vessel. The glaze failed to adhere to the treated surfaces, and because the glaze was by nature viscous it did not run down when melted over the waxed or oiled panels, while the dressing itself was dissipated in the heat of the kiln without leaving any trace of its application. The result was quite as satisfactory as that attained by the use of floated reliefs. The use of a resist, to give the new method its correct name, seems to have been confined to one, or at most two kilns, neither of them using the floating technique. The stylistic divergence between the two types is sufficient even in the absence of archaeological evidence to justify this conclusion.

No better or more telling example of the type can be presented as evidence of this new treatment than the octagonal *mei-p'ing* in the David Foundation (Plate 66); this can perhaps be dated to the first half of the fourteenth century, and almost certainly after the introduction of unglazed floated reliefs on a horizontal surface. This vase fulfils the criteria of Yüan form, being heavily constructed, with a robust contour and a certain roughness of finish round the foot, so prevalent a feature of the period in the celadons, and a certain elaboration of detail, which is also fairly characteristic. Pressed out, almost certainly in a two-part mould and luted together vertically, the decoration of flower sprays in panels set out in bands above and below a central band of panels enclosing either figures among clouds or chrysanthemum sprays, it displays some of the best qualities of Yüan, in the neatness of detail combined with a strength well-rooted in the new tradition. The central band of panels alone, that included the figures, have been treated with a resist and show up boldly in brick red against the glaucous green of the thick slightly opaque celadon glaze. Proof of the use of a resist is clearly visible in one or two of the panels, where small passages have been missed by the resist painter's brush, and to these adhere spots of celadon glaze. At one time these unglazed panels were gilt, as traces of gold are apparent in many places. While gilding was not uncommon in the Yüan period, there is no proof that these areas were habitually so embellished, or even in this instance that they were gilt at the time of manufacture. The fact that other examples belonging to the same family of vases, such as the one in the British Museum, and that in the Cleveland Museum of Art, show no trace of this additional ornament, but rather of colouring matter, is ample warning against making such an assumption.

To the same group, and from the same kiln as the octagonal vases, belongs a more unusual example of the resist technique in combination with moulding. This is an octagonal stem-cup of remarkably angular profile, decorated on the flaring outer faces with designs of herons in lotus pools, each panel with a slightly different design (Plates 67A, B). On the inside are the Eight Buddhist emblems and in the centre the character *fu*, 'happiness', with cloud elements, all in moulded relief under the glaze. Wherever this stem-cup and the *mei-p'ing* vases were made, it is clear that they belong to a group having closely related and easily distinguishable designs. The unusual curly cloud form is found, too, on a series of dishes and plates, all of them with a central motif of either a semi-reclining cow-like beast, referred to by Wirgin as the *hsi-niu* rhinoceros (Plate 68A)[1] or with a stag on whose back is a saddle surmounted by an apparently smoking vase (Plate 68B). The glaze on these tends to be thinner, more transparent and glassy than on most other pieces, and the body material, though burnt the usual reddish brown where exposed on the foot, is appreciably paler, showing a pale greyish-white through the glaze where it runs thin over the higher parts of the relief decorated areas. These plates, with their flattened rim and bracket-lobed edge, are quite different in style from many others of the period and have no con-

[1] J. Wirgin, *Sung Ceramic Designs*, Stockholm, 1970, pp. 196–8.

nection with those on which the decoration has been sprig-moulded. The cloud forms, too, are remote from those seen, for instance, on the David flask (Plate 63), and the chrysanthemum and peony scrolls that encircle the well are unrepresented among the products of other celadon kilns; in their drawing, indeed, the closest relatives in style would seem surprisingly enough to be the blue and white and some of the moulded white wares from Chi-chou. The carefully calculated design, the bracket foliation and the curly cloud motifs, all based on multiples of four, indicate that this group should be dated slightly after the middle of the fourteenth century, and almost certainly later than the greater number of pieces with floated reliefs.

Among other mould-constructed pieces at this time, but differing in style, is a handsome *mei-p'ing* formerly in the Russell Collection (Plate 69). Decorated with four large panels round the central area, each enclosing plantain and rock designs alternating with a peacock or peahen on a peony branch, and bordered on the shoulder by a lotus scroll, and below by a double band of palmettes, one pendant and the other erect, it displays all the boldness and largeness of scale that so emphatically characterizes the best products of the age. The deep moulding has its nearest parallels in a number of massive wine jars on which are large-scale pictorial designs round the central field, with broad plantain leaf bands, sometimes alternating with lotus petals in a band below. The scenes in the main band may, like some of those on the blue and white, have been taken from the illustrations of contemporary drama, and thus date from the middle and later years of the Yüan period.[1] These jars are frequently heavy and often carelessly constructed of a paste that tends to be coarse. The base in many instances follows the pattern seen in the vase of 1327, with the whole area cut out and covered from the inside with a saucer sealed in place with glaze. Very late examples, likely to date from the end of the fourteenth century, are less well moulded and the base is usually left intact.

Any relationship there may be between this rather sombre, heavy moulded type, whatever the quality, and the persistently finer-quality carved celadon wine jars, seems to be fairly remote. The only links that can be discerned are those of body and glaze, both of which in fact are common to the whole industrial area. The peony leaf alone, which may possibly be connected with the type found on such massive wine jars as that in Philadelphia (Plates 70A, B, C), is too tenuous a link on which to construct a valid relationship. These massive jars, with a petal band round the bottom, a boldly carved scroll often on a hatched ground, and heavy, wide, domed cover belong to a large

[1] Kikutaru Saito, *Gendai no sometsuke* ('Yüan blue and white'), *Kobijutsu*, 18, 1967. Japanese text with English summary.

group of rather varied pieces, most of them constructed on the same massive form, which appear closely related to the 1327 vase (Plate 58), and they are characterized by an accomplished style of carving, which impresses one by its fluency. Some of these are likely to be very near in date to the famous Ta-yao vase and it seems probable that they were all made there in the succeeding years. A handsome dish about 30 cm. across (Plate 71) is an interesting member of the same family. The foot-ring is square-cut and stout, and is glazed over. Within the foot-ring is an unglazed band about 2.5 cm. wide running all round, and the rest of the base is glazed, a feature fairly common to the larger celadon plates at this time. In the centre is a single boldly carved pomegranate spray, with a few crisp incisions in the leaves which increase the definition and fill out the design. Round the well is a fluently and spontaneously sketched scrolling design, perhaps an abstraction from a leaf scroll, and round the flattened rim is a tersely treated classic scroll, one of the few examples of the use of this motif in the Lung-ch'üan celadons. Somewhat similar to this dish and probably a little later is a handsome basin of very large proportions in the David Foundation (Plates 72A, B). In this example the pomegranate flowers, decorating the upper area of the inside, have deteriorated and instead of firmly cut defining lines on the petals, as in the Locsin dish, there are a few mechanically placed digs in the surface; the leaves too have changed, being schematically treated to resemble something approaching a scroll. Round the upper part outside is an abstracted scrolling design similar again to that on the Locsin dish, but now slightly abbreviated. Immediately below the rim on the outside a new element has been introduced, the angular meander, while below the scroll is a band of petal panels, another fairly new motif to the celadons.[1] The base, like that of so many large fourteenth-century pieces, has been cut away and the aperture covered from the inside. In this instance the sealing element is a relief-moulded flower of chrysanthemum type; an inverted saucer would scarcely have been appropriate in such a vessel.

At this point, fairly near the middle of the century, or perhaps just after, we come face to face with what appears to be cross-fertilization from Jao-chou and the blue and white repertory of design. The true lotus scroll is introduced into the well of a large plate (Plate 73), the main elements being carefully placed and linked by a cursively drawn leaf-type scroll. In this Topkapu Seray plate there is again the angular meander, now remarkably precisely drawn. The most vivacious

---

[1] The appearance of this motif on the basin provides a useful link with some of the spouted bowls, especially that formerly in the Fujita Collection, referred to in footnote 1, p. 69.

drawing on the dish is reserved for the dominating central element of a pair of fish in the midst of a highly individual wave pattern. The conception of the floral scroll is further developed in a typical Yüan manner in a plate in the Locsin Collection, the scroll being carried round the well in total disregard of the fluted well.[1] As in the earlier strata of blue and white the number of bracket foliations was awkward, so too is this to be seen in the larger plates in the Lung-ch'üan series. In the case of the Locsin plate the number is fourteen, a number also to be found in Group 2 of the blue and white, and a difficult one to work out in a satisfactory manner.[2] It is peculiarly strange in this plate that such a number should have been used, because the central motif is quatrefoil, though rather roughly executed. By the end of the century, however, the development of the type is complete, as may be seen in the massive plate in the Topkapu Seray (Plate 74). Not only has the Jao-chou repertory here been completely accepted, but numerical symmetry has also been absorbed. The lotus pool in the centre, the radially disposed flower sprays in the well and the rather elaborate classic scroll are all correctly assembled and placed on the plate with its sixteen bracket foliations and corresponding fluting in the well.[3] The intricate design does not perfectly suit the carving technique, but the interest of the potters of one area in the productions of those of another is strikingly shown in this example of perhaps the last quarter of the fourteenth century. A similar interest is shown in the highly accomplished and aesthetically more successful bottle-shaped vase, which was first shown in Venice in 1954 (Plate 75). This vase displays precisely the same features that are apparent in the contemporary underglaze red painted ones, with certain necessary modifications to suit the carving technique, such as a wider spacing of the key-fret and a slight reduction in the number of lappets at the top of the central band. The free drawing of the vine and the admirable proportion of this to the surface combine to make the vase a particularly memorable example of the Lung-ch'üan potter's art. Even the form adheres closely to the proportions current at the end of the century at Jao-chou. A large ewer in the Topkapu Seray, which perhaps dates from the beginning of the fifteenth century, displays similar features, though slightly less well executed.

One other group of celadons deserves special mention, because it continues a fashion that began in the Southern Sung period and is common to both Lung-ch'üan and Kuan. This consists of the vessels

---

[1] L. and C. Locsin, *Oriental Ceramics discovered in the Philippines*, Figure 126.
[2] See above, p. 42.
[3] Ernst Zimmermann, *Altchinesische Porzellane im alten Serai* (*Meisterwerke der türkische Museen zu Konstantinopel*, Band 2), Berlin and Leipzig, 1930, Tafel 6.

of archaic bronze form, which became popular after the retreat of the Chinese from the north to the new capital at Hang-chou in 1128. It is in the archaic bronze forms imitated in the Lung-ch'üan wares that we discover the only possible means of linking the light-grey bodied celadons to the crackled glaze, dark bodied type associated with Kuan wares. This raises the question of what constitutes a body of Kuan wares that can be attributed to the Yüan period, a question which will take much time and study to settle. While it may be possible to suggest that particular specimens, especially of archaic bronze or jade shapes, are likely to belong to the Yüan period on the basis of analogy with the Lung-ch'üan celadons, no great mass of material can at present be assigned to the late thirteenth and fourteenth centuries except on the most speculative grounds. The root of the problem lies in the fact that there is no evidence as to the length of time during which the Chiao-t'an kiln at Hangchou continued in operation. Similarly there is no published evidence on the centre of manufacture of Lung-ch'üan imitations, on which Dr. Ch'ên Wan-li has expressed his opinion to the effect that it is virtually impossible to distinguish the difference between the genuine Chiao-t'an products and imitations from the Lung-ch'üan region.[1] Moreover we have with us the perennial problem of the Kuan type described as Hsiu-nei Ssŭ, to which there is nothing to be added or subtracted at the present juncture. Gompertz has dealt fairly with this controversial subject, and his account of the position, published in 1958, remains unchanged, and is likely so to remain unless some entirely unexpected archaeological evidence comes to light.[2] This does not mean that no pieces at all can be attributed to the late thirteenth or fourteenth centuries; as suggested above a link between the two wares is provided by the common interest in archaic bronze forms. There are also a number of other pieces of Kuan which appear not to fulfil our conceptions of what constitutes Sung criteria and are at the same time divergent from examples that are generally recognized as Ming or Ch'ing copies made in the Jao-chou area. These divergent pieces are likely to include the more heavily constructed examples, such as we are accustomed to expect in the Yüan period, in addition to some of the archaic types, which we consider first.

The archaic bronze forms most commonly represented in the ceramic medium are those which in fact have their ultimate origin in clay, so it is not surprising to find the *hu*, *tsun*, *ku*, *kuei* and *li*, as well perhaps as the *ting* forms included in the repertory. Of these forms,

[1] See footnote 1, p. 63. It is, however, stated that imitations were made near Chi-k'ou, but no comparative material has so far been published.

[2] Gompertz, op. cit., pp. 42–3.

the *kuei* and the *li* are common to Kuan and Lung-ch'üan, the *hu* is found only in Kuan, and the *tsun*, *ku* and *ting* are confined to Lung-ch'üan. If we take first the forms common to both wares we find that the *kuei* is differently treated in the two areas, the Lung-ch'üan examples tending to adhere more closely to the metal prototype. It is particularly important to notice that the nearest equivalent to the Lung-ch'üan treatment of the *kuei* shape in Kuan wares is the hexagonal one in the David Foundation (Plate 76B). This stands out immediately as atypical both as a Kuan piece and as one of the Sung date. Both in size and in angularity of contour it marks such a sharp departure from the suave lines of the Kuan tradition that a revised dating to the Yüan period, and probably in the fourteenth century, seems wholly appropriate. In addition the introduction on this vessel of the Eight Trigrams as a decorative motif would also suggest a later date, for the use of this rather uninteresting element in the vocabulary of ceramic ornament does not seem on present evidence to antedate the fourteenth century; in metalwork its earlier appearance is limited to a few late T'ang and tenth-century bronze mirrors. The more usual *kuei* form in Kuan is a smaller, rounder type with handles of a quite different kind and seems to have been popular over a longer period. The persistence of the form into the fourteenth century is perhaps implied by the discovery of one such piece in a Yüan tomb in the province of Kiangsu.[1] There are a number of similar examples to this in the David Foundation and most of them include a feature which in recent years has been suggested as a post-Sung element; this is the use of spurred stands. As yet there is no evidence from which to conclude that spurs were not used in late Sung times, about the middle of the thirteenth century. Since there is a surprisingly large number of pieces fired in this way, it seems likely that the use of spurred stands does pre-date the fall of the dynasty.

The *li* form, which is also common to Kuan and Lung-ch'üan, presents a grave difficulty owing to the paucity of Kuan examples. The only one it has been possible to examine closely is the very small specimen, and a waster at that, which Sir Percival David picked up on the site of the Chiao-t'an kiln when he visited Hang-chou in company with Hobson. This has a dark body and crackled glaze, and is constructed in exactly the same way as one of the much larger Lung-ch'üan examples also in the Foundation which, on the basis of the construction, might well be later than Sung.[2] If this is in fact the case,

[1] *Kiangsu Shêng ch'u-t'u wên-wu hsüan-chi* ('Selected objects from excavations in Kiangsu'), Peking, 1963, Plate 193.
[2] No. 285. The vents for the legs are cut as rough holes in the bottom of the bowl, unlike the neater and, I believe, earlier type in which the vents are almost invisible, being on the underside and consisting of quite small nail-head sized holes.

it gives strong support for the supposition that the Chiao-t'an kiln continued its activity well beyond the end of the Sung dynasty. This would seem to be borne out, too, by the very large Kuan *hu* in the David Foundation, which is of unusually heavy construction, the foot appearing to have been added separately, a characteristic feature of a number of Yüan types. The vessel, which cannot be classed a great masterpiece, in spite of the Ch'ien-lung inscription inside the mouth, is covered with a dull almost brown glaze, with only a few parts showing any traces of the pale greyish blue or green that one associates with the best of Kuan. The body, where this is exposed is less obviously dark, but this may be due to an ill-controlled firing.[1] The vessel raises the question whether this is a genuine Kuan example, with rather close crackle, or whether it is a mis-fired Lung-ch'üan imitation.

When it comes to the *tsun* and *ku* forms there is no such difficulty; both shapes are clearly Lung-ch'üan celadon, having a pale grey stoneware or porcellanous body burning the usual reddish brown where exposed on the foot-ring. Both shapes are more solidly constructed than one would expect of the Sung tradition in this area. This is especially true of the *tsun*, and both forms should probably be attributed to Yüan, though they may be early in the period (Plate 77).

Finally there is a small group of Kuan pieces, apart from those of archaic bronze shape, which seem possible candidates for a Yüan date. These are nearly all small vessels and include those which we call brush-washers; they are invariably fired on spurs, the glaze having been carried over the small ridge which in other pieces would be left free as a foot-ring (Plate 76A). There are also some small rather heavily made saucers, some of them rectangular, with a dull greyish or even brownish glaze and a close very dark crackle. The dating of such pieces as these presents almost insuperable difficulties, if only because of the popularity of these forms and their extensive use by members of the educated class probably over an extended period. Moreover Chinese literature persistently informs us that there are broadly four types of Kuan, the best being pale greenish in colour with 'crab's claw' marking, the second quality being a pronounced grey with an irregular marking, the third quality being very pale with a fine dark crackle, and the fourth and last being dull grey with a close irregular crackle.[2] As much of the material available belongs to the lower quality groups, we may well be justified in entertaining doubts on dating any Kuan

---

[1] The body of Lung-ch'üan wares varies greatly from one kiln to another and the same forms from different kilns, or even from the same one, reflect this so that it is justifiable to use both terms.

[2] Chu Yen, *T'ao-shuo*, 1775; see Bushell's translation, *Descriptions of Chinese Pottery and Porcelain*, Oxford, 1910, pp. 41–3.

at all. These lower-quality wares are the types formerly described as Ko, a term now generally discarded.[1] The justification for ridding ceramic terminology of this confusing name is strongly supported by the description of the wares given in the *Ko-ku yao-lun*, the earliest text, of late fourteenth-century date, to describe it.[2] To make the suggested attributions to the Yüan period is to open up anew the whole question of the chronology of Kuan, and clearly the re-assessment of the large body of surviving material is a task to be undertaken in the future.

[1] Oriental Ceramic Society exhibition, *Ju and Kuan wares: Imperial wares of the Sung dynasty*, introduction by Sir Percival David, *T.O.C.S.*, 27, 1951–53.

[2] Ts'ao Chao, *Ko-ku yao-lun*, 1388. Translated and annotated by Sir Percival David as *Chinese Connoisseurship*, London, 1971, published posthumously, p. 139.

5

NORTHERN CELADON, CHÜN
AND TING

Fifteen years ago it would have seemed absurd to attribute more than
a handful of rather degraded and debased specimens of the products
of the kilns in north China to the period of Mongol rule. The Chinese,
however, in the period following the establishment of the Communist
regime over the whole country in 1947, have carried out a very large
number of investigations of kiln sites in Honan, Hopei, Shansi and
Shensi, which have yielded many interesting and valuable results,
some of the finds being unequivocally assignable to the Yüan period.[1]
Even in the reports published during the last twenty years, there has
nevertheless appeared a certain reluctance among some writers to
give the Yüan its due weight, and this is only partly due to the
uncertainty of much of the evidence. It has often happened that even
in discussing problems of chronology, there has seemed to be a certain
aversion in the published reports to mentioning the dynasty at all, so
that the reader leaps directly from Sung to Ming; even Chin is ignored.
This apparently ingrained habit of refusing to allow any foreign
dynasty adequate recognition for its cultural contributions to the mainstream of Chinese history forces the art historian into an unenviable
position, virtually compelling him to draw conclusions which are at
present almost impossible to verify. While a few of the reports on
excavations do admit the existence of both Chin and Yüan, the
problems to be faced in these northern areas are very real, and are
obstacles in the way of making fair judgements on the course taken in
the evolution of forms and decorations as they occurred at different
centres. Much reading between the lines of rather summary archaeological reporting necessarily increases the margin of error, because

[1] For a list of excavations from 1947 to 1965 see Fêng Hsien-ming's 'Important
finds of ancient Chinese ceramics since 1949', summarized in translation from
Wên-wu, 1965, No. 9, pp. 26–56 in *O.C.S.*, *Chinese Translations*, No. 1, London,
1967.

speculation within certain limits is almost unavoidable. Revisions, constant and perhaps fundamental, should therefore be expected in the future with regard to what is stated and suggested in the following pages, despite the fact that a pattern, albeit a slightly uncertain one, does emerge.

Although the destruction of some centres was undoubtedly a consequence of the invasion of the Chin Tartars in 1127 and the following year, others more remote from the main trouble spots continued in production. A somewhat similar pattern was repeated in the early years of the thirteenth century following on successive waves of invasion by the Mongols, but with one or two significant differences. Nevertheless, excavations so far reported show that a few of the economically richer and artistically more lively kilns succeeded in maintaining their output, and even in some cases increasing it, over a long period, one or two of them even through the whole of the fourteenth century into the early years of the Ming dynasty, though often there was a falling off in terms of quality.

Of the wares with which we are concerned here, the Northern Celadon, Chün and Ting are the main ones, Tz'ŭ-chou being treated separately on account of its great variety in the following chapter. Northern Celadon almost certainly perished before the end of the Mongol period as our knowledge of the kilns stands at the present time. Chün was to continue in some centres and in a modified form into the Ming dynasty, and the Ting, the only high-quality pure white bodied ware of importance in the north in the Sung dynasty, was like Northern Celadon to come to an end in the fourteenth century. It is noteworthy that the kilns which seem to have survived longest were those in Honan, nearer to the main internal trade routes than those of Shensi, where the famous Yao-chou celadon kilns were situated, and in Hopei and northern Honan where Tz'ŭ-chou had its primary centres of production.

NORTHERN CELADON

The grey bodied stoneware covered with a transparent olive green or brownish glaze, to which for so long we have given the name Northern Celadon, was produced at two main centres. One was at Lin-ju Hsien in the province of Honan lying south-east of the old capital of Lo-yang and south-west of the Sung capital at K'ai-fêng on the Yellow river.[1] The excavations that have taken place at this site have not so far been very extensive or systematic and, although they

[1] *Wên-wu*, 1964, No. 8, p. 15 et seq. Earlier and shorter reports also appear in *Wên-wu*, 1951, No. 2; 1956, No. 12; 1958, No. 10.

have covered a fairly wide area, they have scarcely constituted more than a preliminary survey of a potentially very rich archaeological area. Little if any of the celadon material from this site can be ascribed with certainty to the Yüan period, unlike that found at the other major site. This is at Yao-chou in Shensi, about seventy-five miles north of Ch'ang-an, the T'ang dynasty capital on the Wei river. The kilns at Yao-chou in modern Tung-ch'üan present a very different picture and the excavations, of a systematic nature and generally speaking well-reported, have brought to light evidence the significance of which cannot be over-estimated.[1]

The situation of these kilns in Shensi was convenient in as much as there was an almost inexhaustible supply of most of the raw materials needed. The clays required were of good quality, and the coal supply was easily accessible as well as apparently unlimited. The lines of communication were good, there being a reasonably well-maintained road southwards to the Wei river, which was suitable for light river traffic. With these advantages it is to be expected that the pottery produced would not only be of good quality, but would also be in wide demand. It can in fact be inferred from the site and the quantities of remains that ceramics were for Yao-chou an exceptionally profitable commodity. The kilns had been established first in the later years of the T'ang dynasty, producing at that time white glazed stonewares, some with black painting on slip,[2] black wares, some yellowish glazed ware and a small quantity of greenish glazed wares which were probably the immediate precursors of the Northern Celadon with which we are familiar today. It was, however, only in the Sung dynasty that there began that concentration on celadon that made the kilns famous throughout north China, so that in the last years of the eleventh century and the first part of the twelfth century they were able to lay claim to imperial patronage. In the period from 1102 to 1106, for instance, it is recorded that the kilns sent 112,627 pieces of the ware to the Chinese capital at K'ai-fêng.[3]

The Chin invasion of north China in 1127–28 undoubtedly forced some recession, but new kilns were soon opened up farther up the hillside and up the road to the north of the main sites close to the river, and in the next few years production increased and continued almost unabated at these until well into the Yüan period of occupation which began about a century later. While the forms current in the

[1] *Shensi T'ung-ch'üan Yao-chou yao* ('Excavations of Yao-chou kiln sites at T'ung-ch'üan, Shensi'), Peking, 1965. In Chinese with English abstract.
[2] The T'ang material from the site has not been completely published, but the black painted wares would appear to be precursors of the painted Tz'ŭ-chou type.
[3] *Sung-shih* ('Dynastic history of Sung'), Chüan, 87, f. 2a (*Ssŭ-pu pei-yao* edition).

E. *Celadon plate with relief dragon in biscuit. Diam.* 45·1 *cm.*
Percival David Foundation

Sung period were for the most part to remain virtually unchanged, the decorations employed naturally developed and were gradually transformed until in the Yüan they bore little resemblance to the originals from which they were descended. The basic techniques appear to have undergone very little change and it seems as though the same type of kiln was used throughout the Sung and right through to the end of the period of activity. The most important results of the excavations carried out here were, first, the discovery of nine kilns, of which a group of three set one alongside another, proved of the greatest interest, and second, the discovery of phenomenal amounts of kiln equipment, and moulds and wasters with their decorations sufficiently intact to make possible the recognition of a very extensive repertory of designs which can be arranged in a series of chronological groupings.

From the technical point of view the discovery of the kilns themselves has proved immensely instructive. For the first time it has been made possible to reconstruct a northern Chinese down-draught kiln for reduction firing with a high degree of accuracy. All the kilns found were of what the Chinese call 'horse-shoe shaped' variety. One of the kilns found, that could be reconstructed, was a simple one intended for the firing of saggars and had none of the special refinements necessary for the successful reduction firing. In the group of three set out in line and intended for firing the finished wares, however, the middle one of the group was sufficiently well preserved to make complete reconstruction possible. Roughly semi-circular in shape, the kiln is divided into three main parts, a fire-box in the centre of the arc facing the diameter of the semi-circle, a main chamber widening out from the fire-box to the widest points on either side, and a third section beyond this and cut off from it by a massive wall is the chimney stack; connecting the main chamber and the chimney stack compartment is a row of vents set at the base of the wall. The circumference wall, sunk into the ground, rises to a height of several feet. At this point reconstruction has to be undertaken. If the conventional structure of such a kiln is adhered to, as seems likely it was, the main roof would have been of fairly light construction and dome-shaped; it would be of light construction because it was usually necessary to demolish and rebuild the roof at regular intervals on account of its deterioration at high temperatures. After the stacking of the kiln preparatory to firing, a wall of the type known as a 'bag wall', a light firebrick structure, had to be built between the fire-box and the stacked firing chamber; this would reach up about two-thirds of the height of the chamber. Without this the heat of the fire would have been drawn directly through the stacked wares to the vents at the

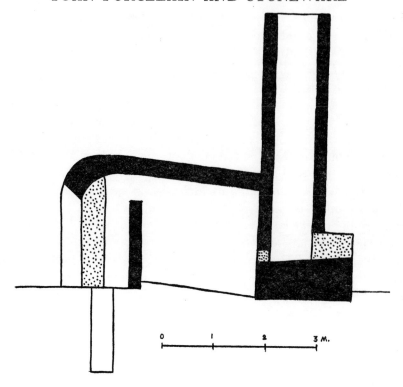

ELEVATION OF THE YAO-CHOU KILN

base of the chimney stack at the far side of the chamber (see text figure). With the bag wall constructed in the correct place and up to the proper height, the heat would be carried up over the top and then forced downwards by the domed roof toward the vents at the far side and into the chimney, the heat being distributed fairly evenly through the stacked wares. The quality of the finished article was largely dependent upon two factors, the correct stacking of the kiln so that the flame and heat could circulate evenly, and the proper timing and control of the reduction firing cycle, so as to produce the characteristic olive or grey-green when using the correctly balanced glaze formula. Such a kiln could be fired equally well with wood or coal, but the Yao-chou kilns seem usually to have been fired with coal, as large quantities of coal clinker have been found not only on the rubbish heaps, but also in the fire-boxes of the kilns.

The value of the discovery of moulds and wasters at Yao-chou is of the greatest significance, since they provide the means whereby we can construct a comprehensive framework for the dating of the celadons of north China by both technique and style from early Sung right through Chin and to the end of commercial activity in the Yüan.

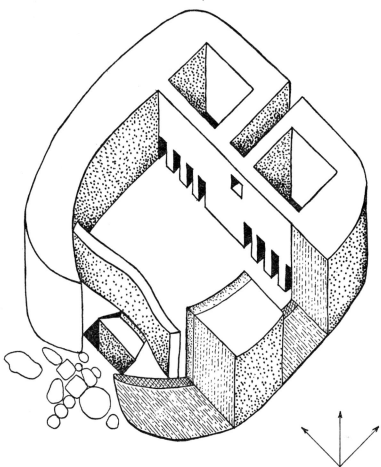

ISOMETRIC RECONSTRUCTION OF THE YAO-CHOU KILN

Besides the kilns, refuse heaps and pits, the workshop areas of the
Chin and Yüan kilns at Huang-pao-chên, Li-ti-po and Shang Tien-
ts'un, the three most productive groups in the area furnish additional
evidence of this thriving industry, but it is undoubtedly the finds of
moulds and wasters that are most important. The archaeologists were
able within limits to establish a stratification, although this was not
always too clearly defined or perhaps correctly interpreted by the
Chinese in the report; it does, however, offer a means of identifying
and dating much material now to be seen in both public and private
collections throughout the world with some likelihood of accuracy.

The distinction between Yüan and earlier wares from Yao-chou is
to a large extent one of quality, but there are also substantial differences in the treatment of the decoration; the forms used are generally
very similar to those of the Sung and Chin in the twelfth century. In

quality the difference is most noticeable in the tendency towards heaviness of form and to oxidation in the firing, the latter leading to a loss of green in the glaze in favour of brownish or yellowish tones, often with a degree of opacity not found in the earlier wares. Northern Celadons are in any case rather inconsistent as to both colour and translucency of glaze, but this now becomes more pronounced and on some pieces the glaze is almost completely opaque. This is likely to be due very largely to poor preparation of the ingredients and to a failure to maintain close control of the firing cycle, or underfiring, or both, and not to a variation in the proportions of the constituents of the glaze, which can be adjusted within surprisingly wide limits without having obvious effects on the finished piece.

Many of the decorations continue the tradition that had been established during the twelfth century, in which moulded designs of infants sporting among flowers had begun to play an important part (Plates 78A, B). The glaze is now sometimes thinner than previously, and in poorly fired examples it is apt to draw away from those parts of the design that stand in relief, a defect that is given even greater emphasis when the glaze also displays degradation. This is a fault with moulded pieces and is rarely seen on carved or incised specimens, which in both Chin and Yüan show a marked diminution in numbers.

A particularly good example of the late style in the carved type is the bowl in the Barlow Collection (Plate 79A) which may be dated to the middle or late thirteenth century; it has a thinner and better controlled glaze of even olive brown than is found on many specimens. Examples of the type were found in the Chin/Yüan levels at Yao-chou, but the Barlow bowl has an unglazed ring in the centre, which is evidence of the common Yüan practice of stacking bowls one on top of another, suggesting the later period for the manufacture of this particular specimen. Another bowl among the relatively small number of carved pieces of the period is also in the Barlow Collection. More rounded in shape than the former one with its restricted rim, it is decorated only on the inside with what is described by Sullivan as 'a mythical animal among plants set in a square cusped medallion',[1] with scrolling elements to fill out the design so as to fit the circular surface (Plate 79B). The rather glassy green glaze is closely crazed and shows brown staining, a not uncommon feature of the later examples with transparent glaze on a rather heavy body. A design similar to this, which is perhaps slightly earlier in date, of a *hsiu-nu* rhinoceros and a crescent moon with foliage elements was found in the Chin/Yüan levels at

[1] Michael Sullivan, *Chinese Ceramics, Bronzes and Jades in the Collection of Sir Alan and Lady Barlow*, p. 137, C.198.

Huang-pao-chên, the most prolific kiln group of the thirteenth and early fourteenth century. This rather large-scale simple manner of carving seems characteristic of the later group, the refined and rather smaller scale designs planned to fill the whole surface characteristic of the late eleventh century and the early years of the twelfth century being left behind; but this is not the only change. It is perhaps the most striking difference between the early twelfth-century pieces and those of the early part of the following century, that in the latter period not only are moulded pieces in an over-whelming majority, but that the quality of the moulding has under-gone so noticeable a change. Late Northern Sung moulding is crisp and clean and the resulting object, even when quite thickly glazed, can often be mistaken at first sight for a carved example. By the thirteenth century the moulds had become less keen and the outlines of the elements making up a design are consequently softer, blurred and less emphatic, a characteristic to which attention is inevitably drawn by the additional blurring of the contours due to the increased opacity of the glaze and a tendency towards a matt surface, probably due to bad firing control, if not to underfiring. With the passing of time the mass-production method of moulding, less exacting in its demands on both skill and time, had become the standard method of manufacture. Not only was this rapid and less skilled method employed, but as time went on it became normal practice, as stated above, to stack the bowls and dishes on top of one another in the same saggar (Plates 80A, B). This naturally involved leaving an unglazed ring in the bottom of the vessel so that another could rest on it without the risk of the pieces sticking together. Needless to say this method of stacking sometimes went wrong and a pile of pieces would be found all stuck together in the saggar. The method undoubtedly saved space in the kiln, but added nothing to the attraction of the pieces. The impli-cation of this method of production is that the kiln managers found themselves under economic pressure to maintain a high level of production at a low cost. The practice at this time was by no means confined to Yao-chou, but because of the recovery of such great quan-tities of wasters in the excavations, it appears more obvious here than in other areas.

The forms of bowls remain standard with the conical bowls, slightly flared or everted at the rim, being probably the most common. But there are others with a straight slightly thickened rim, and others still that are flatter and more like small dishes, a few of which could be described as saucers. The moulded decoration on a great number of the small dishes is restricted to a band encircling the unglazed ring near the centre. Sometimes the decoration consists of a naturalistically drawn lotus scroll and sometimes of sprays of lotus and other flowers alternating in six panels into which the surface is divided by low ribs. An example of the former, with somewhat yellowish brown glaze on a coarse buff body is in the Victoria and Albert Museum (Plate 80B), one very close indeed to a find from Yao-chou.

The deeper bowls with flared rim seem more varied in their decoration, children sporting among floral scrolls and ducks and lotus on a water hatched ground being two popular designs, with chrysanthemum and other floral scroll decorations also occurring frequently. Most of the bowls so far known, and which it has been possible to identify as belonging to this late period, are small, rarely more than about 13 cm. in diameter, but among the excavated material some rather larger examples of about 20 cm. have been found, so we may in the future, as we become more familiar with the types and styles, be able to attribute what have hitherto been seen as problem pieces to the thirteenth and fourteenth centuries, and perhaps even to Yao-chou. The excavation report is particularly valuable in this respect as the excellent drawings of the designs recorded make it relatively easy for the eye to distinguish the different stages of development through which the designs passed and to assess the characteristics to be associated with the different periods.

The provision of this repertory of design means, too, that while we may continue to use the generic term Northern Celadon as a matter of convenience, if of little or no justification, we shall more and more in the future make use of the kiln names in identifying the material, a much more satisfactory method of reference and one of valid art historical importance.

CHÜN WARES

A large number of kilns were engaged in the production of Chün type wares, most of them in Honan, the most numerous and closely grouped perhaps being those in the vicinity of Yü-hsien, but there were a number of others also in Hopei, especially in the Chên-ting Fu region farther north, where the output seems to have continued well into the Ming period, though some of the later production included other wares.

The Chün body is subject to wide variation in both colour and texture, and although it may be classified as a stoneware, the firing was not invariably in the stoneware range, that is over 1100 degrees centigrade, so that it would not be incorrect to call some pieces earthenware. The distinction can be ascertained by a simple absorption test on the exposed part of the body. If the water is rapidly absorbed into the body material, then the firing temperature will have been in the earthenware range, below 1100 degrees centigrade. This does not appear to have had any great effect on the character of the glaze, which was perhaps specially balanced when a lower temperature was used or, a more interesting alternative, the body was biscuit fired to the stoneware level and the glaze then fired on at a lower temperature in the second firing. There is some evidence of this latter practice, but not that it was a universal one in force at all centres of production.[1]

The glaze colour and texture, also somewhat variable, may be due to variations in both constitution and firing from one centre to another. This could easily be the case in view of the many kilns engaged in production over a wide area. The differences in the local materials would force the potters to find alternative solutions to problems of glaze fit in each area. Despite the inconsistencies the fundamental character of Chün remained unaltered in the Yüan period, and the use of reduced copper for purple or crimson splashing, which had been introduced in the early twelfth century continued unabated. The forms remained practical, stoutly constructed and stable, and the glaze remained for the most part thick, opaque and greyish blue, with a tendency to form a welt near the foot of the vessel and to pool on the inside of a bowl.

The most common forms are the ordinary bowls with rounded sides and straight rim about 20 cm. across, and the so-called bubble bowls of less than half this size and inverted at the rim. There were also globular jars with short straight necks and loop handles at the shoulder, plates with flattened rim and finally of a less practical nature, except in a religious context, tripod incense burners. The features that distinguish the Yüan specimens from those of earlier times are the manner of glazing, the treatment of the foot and base, and the more persistent use of copper in the glaze, often in such as way as to make it clear that the applications were deliberate and carefully calculated. A special feature of the glaze itself is that in Yüan times it is often marred by blackish brown smudges of ferruginous impurities, which are occasionally so pronounced as to qualify for the denigratory term of 'spit out'. This defect is caused by a failure to levigate the material well enough to eliminate the heavier iron-bearing particles in the

[1] Fêng Hsien-ming, *Honan shêng Lin-ju Hsien Sung-tai Ju-yao i-chih tiao-ch'a* ('Report on the investigation of kiln sites of Ju type ware and Chün ware in Lin-ju Hsien, Honan), *Wên-wu*, 1964, No. 8, pp. 15–26. Summarized translation in O.C.S., *Chinese Translations*, No. 3, London, 1968. It should be noted that the author in this instance points out that pieces were first fired to a fairly low temperature and to the higher temperature in the gloss firing. While this is not unlikely, it could be the other way about; only the firing temperature of the glaze can provide the answer and this is at present a matter under investigation.

clays and glaze constituents. When the defect is so bad as to justify the term 'spit out', it is usually due to one of these iron-laden particles being disgorged from the body material into the encasing glaze at the higher temperature level in the firing, and staining the glaze with a very high concentration of iron oxide over a small area, producing a rusty scale-like effect on the surface.

Bowls of this period are rarely glazed right down to the foot-ring, nor is glaze always applied on the base. The foot-ring itself, if the body is fine in texture, dense and brown in colour, is very neatly cut, often with a chamfer on the inner edge. On pieces such as these, which are of the finest quality, the smooth, admirably controlled glaze on the outside comes closer to the foot-ring than on other coarser bodied specimens. A variant of the bowl form normally found in the Yüan period is represented by an unusual pair in the Baur Fondation. These are almost conical, rather well made with a neatly cut foot-ring burnt orange brown, and with a glazed base. The unusual feature of these is that the wall thickens towards the rim and is then hollowed out, making an abrupt concave groove round the inner wall just below the rim (Plate 81B). The glaze on both comes right down to the foot-ring and is of the smooth lustrous blue type associated with the highest-quality wares, and the copper staining has clearly been applied with some deliberation.

At the other extreme are the bowls with roughly trimmed foot-ring showing a coarse brown or very dark grey, sometimes almost black body, in some instances with a convex base. On these the glaze stops about half-way down the body on the outside, usually in a thick welt; at the same time the glaze, having flowed downwards fairly freely to pool in the bottom of a bowl, leaves only a thin covering at the rim which then reveals the colour of the body. The impression conveyed is of a brown or black band shading delicately to a greyish blue glaze, which is sometimes flecked with white. The effect can be very attractive, especially when the glaze has a smooth glossy surface instead of the more usual orange peel surface texture. Between the two extremes of the best and the worst, the light bodied and dark bodied coarse textured type, there is wide variation, very good glazes sometimes being found on very coarse bodies and vice versa; there appears no rule of any kind.

The tripod incense burner, based on an archaistic bronze *ting* form seems to have become popular during the twelfth century and to have continued in favour until at least some time in the fourteenth century. On these, with their slightly heavy, sometimes ungainly proportions, the glaze reaches well down over the body on the outside leaving the feet just free and exposed. On the underside of the bowl there is usually an unglazed area, especially in the later examples; on these later pieces the glaze may also be omitted on the bottom inside the bowl. Pieces without handles of any kind were probably the first to appear, perhaps about the middle of the twelfth century, and they continue into the Yüan, when side handles of strictly rectangular form were added, often to vertical loop handles set at the junction of the wide neck and swelling shoulder. The upstanding rectangular handles rise well above the flattened mouth-rim (Plate 81A). Some pieces of this kind are ornamented with moulded reliefs sprigged to the body before glazing. Tripods with these rectangular handles are more ungainly and cumbersome looking than those without handles, and can, it must be confessed, be hideously ugly, with a lavish use of applied reliefs and massive areas of copper-purple. The greatest restraint can be shown, however, as on the rare green Chün tripod in Philadelphia Museum of Art, with its low relief dragon medallion and elegant fish-shaped loops at the shoulder from which rise the flat rectangular handles (Plate 82). This is a large piece, fully in accord with Mongol preferences, but as a type these vessels come in a wide range of sizes and qualities; there are indeed some charming minia-tures, like the one in the Baur Collection of only 4 cm. in height, which must be the smallest on record.[1]

The use of copper for glaze transmutations during the twelfth and thirteenth centuries would seem to have increased in popularity on fine quality wares, and during the late thirteenth century especially some very handsome examples appear to have been made. Character-istic of the thirteenth-century type are the jar in the Victoria and Albert Museum (Plate 83A) and the plate in the David Foundation (Colour Plate F), both of them with a controlled use of copper. The plate has a pale body of fine texture, discernible where the glaze lies thin along the contours. The glaze covers the whole base and even the foot-ring, which is no more than a low ridge, and the object has been fired on a five-spurred almost white fireclay stand. The blue of the glaze is an excellent colour, and the copper displays admirable shading through crimson to purple, with a few small patches of bright moss green, where the copper has re-oxidized in the final stages of the firing. The attempt at patterning is peculiar to this later stage of production. The jar shows similar characteristics but the body is browner so that the glaze at the rim is a soft warm brownish tone fading off through an almost colourless stage to blue. The quality of both jar and plate suggest that they belong to that group of high-quality wares that the Chinese archaeologists believe to have been wood fired.[2] A much more

[1] Baur Collection, Geneva, *Chinese Ceramics*, Vol. I, Plate A39.
[2] *Wên-wu*, No. 1964, 8, pp. 29–30.

spectacular example in both size and patterning is the large basin with flattened rim in the Mount Trust Collection, though here the crimson tones of the copper are overshadowed by the very pronounced purplish blue. The unusually large size of this vessel suggests that it should be dated into the fourteenth century; it bears a marked similarity to the massive dishes of the Lung-ch'üan and Ching-tê Chên output of the same period (Plate 83B). Of much less fine quality, but certainly unique among the Chün wares of Yüan is the large *ju-i* shaped head-rest in the Metropolitan Museum, on which, in dull purple brown with crimson to purple haloing against a rather dull blue glaze, appears the single character *shên*, 'head-rest', written in a remarkably bold style (Plate 84B). Such a flamboyant display would have been very distastefully regarded in Sung times and condemned outright as vulgar, but in terms of Yüan aesthetics, so much more robust had become the attitude, this splendidly spontaneous exhibition of near vulgarity was wholly acceptable.

Among the finest of the undecorated Chün, which can without doubt be dated to the Mongol period, and probably to the end of the thirteenth century at the earliest, is the very important spouted bowl in the Baur Collection (Plate 84A). The form announces it to be a product of the Mongol period based on a silver prototype not known before the thirteenth century; specimens in silver have been found in the central Asian and Iranian area and an example is in the Islamic collection at the Victoria and Albert Museum.[1] We have already seen how this spouted bowl form achieved popularity in Lung-ch'üan celadon, *ch'ing-pai* and the decorated porcelains of Jao-chou. Like the David Foundation plate (Colour Plate F), this remarkable and unique Chün piece has been fired on almost white fireclay spurs and it seems that in Chün wares this is fairly certain evidence of a late date. Until this bowl came to light a few years ago, at about the same time as the Chinese began investigating Chün kiln sites, it was not at all certain that the ware was still being made in its traditional style. It was thought of as only the barest possibility, because up to that time there was insufficient evidence on which to build. The belief in the possibility was only based on the existence of the large narcissus bowls and the flower pots and their saucers, the bases of which are impressed with numbers running from one to ten, indicating sizes within a particular pattern.

In both body and glaze the massive, heavy flower pots and the narcissus bowls are quite distinct from the common run of household wares, and indeed appear not to be the same type of ware as Chün at all, though that have always been classified as Chün (Plates 85A, B).

[1] M. Medley, *Metalwork and Chinese ceramics*, p. 15, Plate 14.

Although fragments of numbered Chün have been reported at one centre which produced Chün, there is no definitive evidence as to where these large and complex pieces were manufactured. Technically they indicate a late stage in the development and they certainly continued into the Ming dynasty. The unusual shapes make it clear that they must have been produced by mechanical means and not on the wheel, a fact suggesting an advanced semi-industrial technology. They are clearly made using a complex system of moulds, and until there is evidence of such moulds being found on a kiln site it is not really possible to determine where they were manufactured; the appearance of numbered fragments is not really sufficient evidence on which to base any valid conclusion. As there is evidence in the Ming dynasty that a certain proportion of what was required for the public service in the capital was ordered by number, this supports the view that the type continued into the Ming, but for just how long it is not possible to be sure. From the evidence of the *Ta Ming hui-tien* we know that Chên-ting Fu in Hopei was an area from which numbered wares were ordered, and it may well be that this type of Chün came from kilns in the vicinity.[1] The body is very dense, fine grained and hard and is generally grey or dark grey in colour. The glaze is thick, thicker than that on the domestic wares, and nearly always a strong crimson purple on the outside, with a slight spill of this colour over the rim; only very rarely is purple also seen on the inside of one of these pots or bowls. Even the large basin in the Fogg Museum of Art and the large bowl in the Severance Millikin Collection at Cleveland are the same, with blue inside and the copper trans-mutation only on the outside. The bases of the wares in this group are only thinly glazed and the colour is usually greenish brown with the thick purplish glaze overlying it at the edges, suggesting that the glaze may have been applied in several layers on the outside. It is this thin greenish glaze on the base that the Chinese refer to as the 'body protecting glaze', and state that without it the purple of the main glaze did not mature. There may be some element of truth in this apparently nonsensical statement, for the study of a series of fragments of Chün of late date on which copper has been used suggests that the potters indulged in some strange procedures when they made these wares. A fragment of Yüan date from the collection of Sir Harry and Lady Garner, generously given to the David Foundation for study, shows under the microscope a clearly defined layer close to the body of oxidized copper green, while on the surface, apparently completely separated from this area by the opalescent blue glaze is a thick layer

---

[1] *Ta Ming hui-tien* (Institutions of Ming), Chüan, 194, f. 2b (Wan-li reprint. 2631b).

of reduced copper of the usual crimson purple. The questions posed by the fragment are many and early answers cannot be expected to any of them. Without adequate research material and opportunities to check hypotheses by experimental work the solutions to the problems posed by Chün, especially in the later stages of its development, are likely to elude us. One question to which the Chinese connoisseur and writer on ceramics knew no answer was the reason for the so-called 'worm track marks', so often quoted as evidence of authenticity. It is a technical fault very often seen on the flower pots and narcissus bowls, but rarely if ever on specimens of other types or on pieces of earlier date. The marks are due to 'crawling' in the early stages of the firing of the glaze, which has failed to flow quite evenly, leaving in the cooling small channels of imperfectly sealed surface. There are several causes for this defect, most of them being due to methods of application of the glaze, one of them, and significantly the most common, being the careless application of glaze in several layers.[1] It is noteworthy that this defect is unknown in Kuan wares, the only other ware so far as we know on which the glaze was applied in successive layers. It is perhaps an indication of the high esteem in which Kuan was held, that so much care was taken to ensure a flawless result apart from the deliberate exploitation of crackle. Chün flower pots and bowls were evidently regarded as more common everyday ware in which the total effect in conjunction with function were the ruling factors.

TING

The attribution of Ting ware to the Mongol period is fraught with exceptional difficulties at present, owing to the lack of systematic excavation of the sites, the work so far done having been no more than exploratory.[2] This means that style is almost the only means of establishing even a relative chronology, and this may only be found to be acceptable in very general terms. It will have to cover what could be called Chin or Yüan and perhaps a style lying in some sense between the two and thus be transitional. In each group there may be

[1] Daniel Rhodes, *Clay and Glazes for the Potter*, London, 1958, p. 156, and David Green, *Understanding Pottery Glazes*, London, 1963, p. 70.

[2] Fujio Koyama discovered the kiln sites in 1941 and a summary of his report was published by James Marshal Plumer in *Archives of the Chinese Art Society of America*, Vol. III, 1948–49, pp. 61–6. The sites were subsequently visited by Dr. Ch'ên Wan-li, whose account appeared in *Wên-wu ts'an-k'ao tz'ŭ-liao* 1953, No. 9, p. 91 et seq., in Chinese. A preliminary survey was undertaken in 1958 and reported by Fêng Hsien-ming in *Wên-wu*, 1959, No. 7, p. 67 et seq. A summary translation of the two exploratory excavations which followed this in 1961 and 1962, published in *K'ao-ku*, 1965, No. 8, pp. 394–415, appears in *O.C.S.*, *Chinese Translations*, No. 4, London, 1968.

included carved and incised wares and in each are certainly to be found moulded wares. The most interesting point about the moulded wares is that they can themselves be separated into two stylistically different groups.

If the carved wares are examined first, it will be found that the forms are very limited in their range; they are almost all plates and dishes. The number of bowls with carved decoration that can acceptably be attributed to late Chin or Yüan is exceptionally small, a different situation from that prevailing among the moulded pieces, which show a fairly even balance of forms. It is as though the craftsman was no longer able to control his design on the rounded surfaces such as presented by the inside of a bowl and has instead to have a virtually flat surface on which to wield his knife. There seem to be two basically different types of handling in this fairly small group of plates and shallow dishes.

One treatment is reserved for *ch'ih* dragons and abstract motifs and the other is reserved for floral decorations. The contrast in the two treatments is particularly well illustrated in two pieces in the David Foundation (Plates 86A, B and 87A). The dish with flaring walls and sharp contraction to the foot-ring illustrated in Plates 86A and B, is of particular interest because the use of the incising point and of the slanting blade both occur on the one piece. Wirgin dates this example to Sung-Chin, but for other reasons than those he adduces it would seem more likely to be late Chin.[1] The form itself is not an early one and is in fact more commonly found among the later moulded pieces, often with the foot-ring luted on separately, as was probably done in this case. Moreover the heavy style of carving is markedly different in the lotus scroll which surrounds and intrudes upon the central field, from the style associated with the earlier part of the twelfth century, when the touch was lighter and the craftsman apparently much more sensitive to the form and surface upon which he was working. A further peculiarity of the decoration is that it is confined, and rather badly at that, by two sharply cut lines running round just below the rim on both the inside and the outside. In the earlier pieces of the twelfth century there is sometimes a finely drawn line round the inside of the bowl, but not as a rule on the outside, as indeed it was relatively rare for the earlier pieces to be decorated on the outside. It will be seen on the dish that the treatment employed for the *chih* dragon decoration is nearer to incising than carving in as much as there is very little gouging out of the contours as with a slanting blade, and none at all in the scroll motif round the rim. The incising tool is frequently used with heavy pressure so that there is a notable lack of

[1] J. Wirgin, *Sung Ceramic Designs*, Stockholm, 1970, p. 139, Ti. 27b.

fluency, the strokes sometimes tending to be short and curling. The plates with the two dragons in the centre and the incipient classic scroll on the rim (Plate 87A) is of interest because it demonstrates a feature of design not seen in earlier examples, but which may often be encountered in the thirteenth century. This is the division of the circular field into what are basically two halves with two identical motifs either facing each other or interlocking in some way. The same treatment is common in the later *ch'ing-pai*,[1] and later still in the fourteenth-century white wares, a classic example of which is the white plate with bracket-lobed rim from the Pao-ting hoard (Plate 17). The same treatment is seen in the eight-lobed plate with lotus scroll decoration in the centre and incipient classic scroll in each lobe of the flattened rim in the Freer Gallery of Art.[2] Such differences as there are, are very small with the centre of the plate being given orientation by the use of a seed pod. The practice of bisecting the central field in this way is common especially with dragon, lotus, and phoenix designs, whether the surface is carved and incised, or moulded. The peony and pomegranate are much less obviously treated in this manner, there being in a number of instances very elegant modification as may be seen on the British Museum plate, with its classic scroll on the rim reflecting strongly the metalworking traditions of the late twelfth and thirteenth centuries (Plate 87B).[3] Another example of later date, perhaps well into the thirteenth century, is the bow-lobed plate illustrated by Wirgin and assigned by him to a rather late Chin date.[4] Probably the latest carved and incised piece of all before the plate in the British Museum dated to 1271,[5] is the small dish in the Victoria and Albert Museum, with its single spray of lotus held as a compact design resembling a bouquet by the wide overlap of the slightly frilled leaf (Plate 91A).[6] The motif was a popular one and the form in which it is found varies from one ware to another as well as over a long period. The feature it has in common with the plate of 1271 is the orientation of the design in one direction only, a development of the thirteenth century in the use of floral motifs, but one commonly seen in a wide range of designs in the moulded plates and dishes. It should be added that this is the only feature that the dated plate has in common with other white wares at this time.

With these two basic concepts of decoration in mind, the bisected

[1] Op. cit., p. 62, Cp. 27, Plate 26b.
[2] Op. cit., p. 141, Ti. 29a, Plate 71.
[3] See, for instance, Dr. Bo Gyllensvärd, *Chinese gold and silver in the Carl Kempe Collection*, Stockholm, 1953, p. 113, Plate 53b.
[4] J. Wirgin, op. cit., p. 142, Ti. 31a, Plate 73b.
[5] B. Gray, *Early Chinese Pottery and Porcelain*, London, 1953, Plate 44b.
[6] J. Wirgin, op. cit., Plate 72b.

repeat and the single view orientation, we can turn to moulded plates and dishes and at the same time add one extra feature that was found on the first of the carved dishes considered—this was the overlap into the central area of a major decorative motif (Plate 88B). The two main concepts and this additional one are manifested consistently in a large number of the moulded wares, which can be broadly separated out into two streams, both of them stylistic, and apart from dated moulds, there is no other means than that of style and its development to enable us to assign any example to a specific date. In one stream is a type distinguished by a largeness of scale, approaching in some cases a grandiose treatment, and in the other stream we find the opposite, a smallness of scale and something approaching what some connoisseurs might condemn as 'pretty'. Between the two one occasionally encounters examples in which elements of the second are super-imposed on the former.

The first type, large in scale in terms of treatment of the surface, appears to grow out of the largeness of scale which one primarily associates with the twelfth-century carved wares, when a boldly conceived floral scroll design is freely disposed over the surface. Good examples of this are the bowl in the Museum of Far Eastern Antiquities,[1] the British Museum bowl (Plate 88A) and perhaps the latest in the series and most important of all, the bowl in the Victoria and Albert Museum (Plate 88B). In this last it is worth noticing that the leaves are of the spiked type with bulbous lobes turned back on either side at the base, a type transmitted to the south, where it re-emerges in the fourteenth-century blue and white tradition as a leaf form accompanying the stylized lotus scrolls and sprays inseparable from the southern development. It is worth remarking that all the examples with this rather large-scale design are bowls which are basically conical, and it seems to be a treatment confined to this form. In these three specimens the surface is divided into halves and quarters, in the Victoria and Albert example with a spill over into the centre, or in three parts as in the case of the British Museum piece, which lacks this feature partly perhaps on account of the need for a very small central medallion. Other specimens of the same kind are a bowl in Seattle, with a *ch'ih* dragon in the centre,[2] and another in Stockholm with a three-part division, less rhythmically co-ordinated than the others.[3] A feature common to many of these is the use of the key-fret border, which is most common, or a rather nondescript scrolling element. The latest in the series would certainly seem to be the Victoria and Albert Museum bowl, which has a very clearly defined

[1] Op. cit., p. 146, Ti. 37, Plate 83.
[2] Op. cit., Plate 92a.   [3] Op. cit., Plate 92b.

pattern and a leaf form that leads on into the fourteenth-century style of the south.

Alongside this largeness of scale in design is the much smaller-scale treatment, which seems to owe little or nothing to the tradition of the carved and incised wares. The group appears to be peculiarly well adapted to the moulding technique and most of the examples are to be found among such forms as it would be difficult to throw on the wheel, most, though not all, being plates and large dishes. The tradition and its surface treatment clearly began in the twelfth century, and specimens with bracket lobes or scalloped rims are evidently late. It is into this context that landscape appears as a motif in its own right, the earliest example perhaps being the large dish in the David Foundation with fluted well and rather shallow moulded decoration of geese by a lake with overhanging willow.[1] In the first instance it was probably a plate, that is a vessel with a flattened rim, but this must have been broken at some time and the edge ground down to the line of the fluting; the metal band round the rim is much thicker than it would be on a properly finished piece. Wirgin dates it to the Chin in the twelfth century, a date with which no one is likely to disagree.[2] Later in the twelfth century and in the thirteenth century the moulds became slightly sharper and heavier, though there were always some pieces in which the moulding was handled with great subtlety and sensitivity. Outstanding examples of sensitivity, and of the orientation in one direction only using landscapes or birds are the lobed plates such as the one in the David Foundation (Plate 89B) and the one in the Japanese collection which has so often figured in illustration.[3] It is important to notice that in neither of these pieces does the lobing of the well appear on the back, and that in both cases the rim has been trimmed by hand. Another example, well into the thirteenth century, is the plate, also in the David Foundation, with a scene in the centre of children at play on a garden terrace (Plate 90A). In this case there is no lobing in the well, but it is implied to be so by its division into a series of panels each separated from the next by a very low relief rib. The flower sprays, one to each panel, are of precisely the same type as those on the lobed plate in the Japanese collection and on the one illustrated in Plate 90B. All three pieces belong to the same stream of development, the last described having for a long time been regarded as a Yüan example, perhaps partly on account of the heaviness of its

---

[1] *Illustrated Catalogue of Ting Yao and related white wares in the Percival David Foundation of Chinese Art*, London, 1964, No. 171.

[2] J. Wirgin, op. cit., p. 156, Ti. 54f, Plate 98.

[3] *One Hundred Masterpieces of Chinese Ceramics*, Tokyo, 1960, Plate 49, and *Sekai tōji zenshū*, Vol. 10, Plate 77.

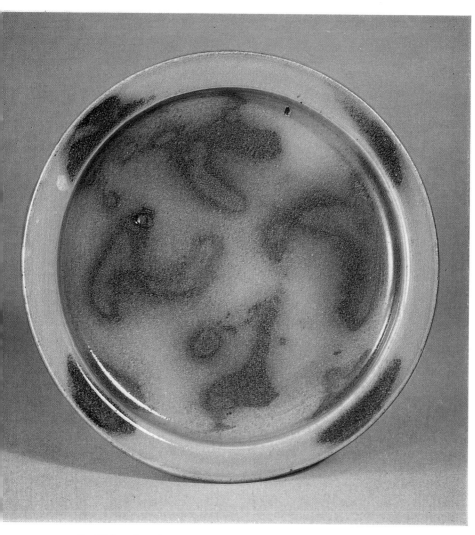

F. *Chün plate, blue with purple splashes. Diam. 18·6 cm.*
Percival David Foundation

construction; it is certainly quite thick and heavy in proportion to its main dimensions and is likely to be later than the lobed examples. In all these pieces the rather small neat flowers are a common denominator as they also are in a large series of plates, dishes and bowls.

Among the bowls with moulded decoration, two examples deserve special mention because each appears to act in its own way as a bridge between the large-scale style and the small-scale style, and one has connexions, though rather remote ones, with a series of carved bowls dating from the twelfth century. One of these two pieces is a bowl in the Clark Collection in which the moulded decoration of a floral scroll resembling the small-scale style, spills over into the central field, an area dominated by two peony flowers (Plate 90B). The bowl itself is six-lobed and in each lobe is an incipient classic scroll. The fact that the wall decoration, which can be divided into four parts, is played against the six lobes of the rim suggests that the bowl should be dated well on into the thirteenth century and thus in the new Mongol tradition. The other bowl, decorated with startlingly similar flowers to those on the Clark bowl as well as to those in the panels round the well of the plate illustrated in Plate 89B, makes this piece another bridge between to the two styles, but it also has a remote connexion in the organization of the surface with an earlier tradition, which itself had links with traced silver bowls.[1] The bowl, an example of this type, decorated with a handsome peony spray in the centre, is encircled by six panels in each of which a double flower spray is spread out to use the available surface from the bottom almost to the six-lobed rim (Plate 89A). There can be little doubt as to the dating of this to the Mongol period and it must be either nearly contemporary or slightly later than the two plates in the David Foundation (Plates 89B, 90A). There is, however, another bowl, also transitional between the two styles, but very different in character, again in the David Foundation. It has rounded walls and vestigial lobing at the rim. It is decorated with a large peony scroll with exceptionally naturalistic flowers, on the leaves and petals of which are superimposed, apparently at random, small prunus florets (Plate 91B). While the Clark bowl may perhaps be dated to the thirteenth century, and closely after it the British Museum bowl, the David one as well as its companion pieces, one of which is in the Victoria and Albert Museum, seems likely to be later still, especially in view of the confused decoration, perhaps into

---

[1] The concept of radiating panels occurs in carved Ting in the twelfth century either as late Northern Sung or early Chin. An example is No. 106 in the David Foundation, *Illustrated Catalogue of Ting Yao etc.*, and in traced silver, the ultimate ancestor, an example may be seen in the bowl illustrated by R. L. Hobson, 'A T'ang silver hoard', *British Museum Quarterly*, Vol. I, Plate IXb.

the fourteenth century. An additional point in favour of the late date may be the quality of the material itself with its iron-stained spots showing through from the body and the rather careless treatment of the outer wall especially in the area close to the rim, which is only roughly finished.

The last group that can be distinguished belongs to a series of small dishes with fluted well and plain or sometimes scalloped rim. Some of these, probably the earliest of them dating from the late twelfth or early thirteenth century, have neat well-executed designs, small in scale and based on a bisected field. Later designs were orientated in one direction only and might include a garden scene, as suggested by Wirgin.[1] The final stage is evidenced by examples in which the scallops may be ornamented with a series of petals of diminishing size, as though laid one on top of one another in each scallop, while the design in the centre becomes a fruit or flower spray. The decoration may vary in the scallop, sometimes with plantain leaves taking the place of petals. In one or two cases the central field is occupied by that strange animal, half-rhinoceros and half-ox, the *hsiu-nu*, gazing soulfully at the moon drifting above on clouds. The best example of this motif, however, is not on a very late thirteenth-century dish with moulded decoration, but on a carved and incised plate with a thickened bracket-lobed rim (Plate 92). The piece probably dates from the second quarter of the thirteenth century, and the design is admirably executed with a stylish water pattern incised across the lower right side sloping away down towards the left of the central field, with the reclining *hsiu-nu* looking back and up over its rump towards the crescent moon. The composition and its execution is of a higher quality than that of other examples and we may suggest that it owes its origin to a popular printed version. Round the well is a finely carved lotus scroll, and the bracket-lobed rim, carefully cut by hand round the flange-like thickening at the edge makes a fitting frame for an exceptional specimen of the early Yüan. In body it bears a slight resemblance to the dated plate of 1271, with its fish and flower, but the dated piece can only be regarded as a northern white type having no associations with the Ting wares. The absence of other material from the Ting sites so far with exactly this type of body, method of construction with the small thick foot-ring, and the thin colourless glaze forbid one to call this even Ting type. No doubt excavations in the future will resolve the problems of the later development of Ting into the fourteenth century, but at the moment the progression into Yüan is anything but clearly defined. There are these various groups which seem to be late, but we are still left with the question, how

[1] J. Wirgin, op. cit., p. 158, Ti. 59, Plate 102a.

late? That the kilns ceased production before the middle of the fourteenth century seems more than likely, unlike the Chün and Tz'ŭ-chou types.

Chün and Tz'ŭ-chou, better placed geographically for marketing and perhaps always more generally popular, were better situated to survive. That both types were able to do so is also a tribute to the ability of the potters to adapt to change in patronage, but there was the added advantage of the kilns being situated on better lines of communication. This is a particularly important factor as regards Tz'ŭ-chou. Unless a kiln area is directly overrun, the invasions by a foreign army or rebellious insurgents would have little effect on production, but the general trends consequent on such an event would in the long term have considerable impact. The Chin after their conquest, for all their desire to acquire Chinese culture which they so much admired, probably had insufficient aesthetic appreciation to provide more than a very limited stimulus to the Ting kilns, which were in any case in a fairly remote region in Chü-yang in the more mountainous part of Hopei, nor could they have had any very great impact on Yao-chou so far away in Shensi beyond the confluence of the Wei and Yellow rivers. This perhaps in Ting, at least, accounts for the persistence of Northern Sung elements right to the end of the twelfth century if not later. For the Chin the products of the more accessible kilns in northern Honan and southern Hopei were infinitely to be preferred. The Yüan pattern so far as the north of China is concerned reveals similar features even after Peking became the administrative capital. Moreover the changing pattern of wealth tended to accelerate the demise of kilns ill-situated geographically to extend any appeal to a wide public, and with the financial benefits, especially of the court draining away, so too would the native inspiration. It was left to the popular taste to stimulate sources of manufacture nearer at hand, and it was those kilns which had in any case always catered predominantly for ordinary folk at the local, conveniently placed markets, that were in the end able to survive the fundamental changes following the break-up of the native dynasty in the north.

The general conclusion is then that the Northern Celadon and Ting, both of them among the most sophisticated ceramic wares of their period, were doomed to perish once enlightened patronage was withdrawn and the main economic focus moved to the south. The final blow came from the Mongols, who, lacking interest in ceramics for their own sake, gave neither encouragement to the potters, nor opportunities in the north for the sort of experimentalism such as that found in the south. The vacuum in the south caused by the collapse of the Sung was immediately filled by the demands of the overseas trade, but in the north the vacuum remained of necessity, since the kilns were too far from the main centres of trade and even farther from the ports. It was thus the shift in economic focus that was ultimately the greatest single factor in bringing to an end the activities of kilns producing the most refined wares, and which forced changes on Chün which virtually transformed it into a new ware.

6

TZ'Ŭ-CHOU AND
RELATED BLACK WARES

The abstraction of Tz'ŭ-chou wares from the continuity of the northern Chinese ceramic tradition for the purpose of subjecting it to special treatment in the Yüan period cannot but strike one as unrealistic, but it is in the present context unavoidable. The character of this largely popular type and its evolution from the time of its inception in the tenth century[1] to its conclusion or transformation in the Ming dynasty merits in its own right a comprehensive and systematic treatment; to review it only in the period from early in the thirteenth to the end of the fourteenth century is to cut across the development at a critical stage. For this reason, and because of the varied decorative treatments in terms of concepts of design and technique of execution, it is not possible to deal fairly here with this important, interesting and deservedly popular type. In the circumstances it seems best to take the main decorative treatments on the basis of the techniques employed and deal with these individually. Such an approach will inevitably result in a series of short disconnected essays, but it will perhaps make more manageable the problem of reference to the great body of surviving material. Before doing this, however, consideration should be given to the background, to the material and to the basic characteristics of forms, designs, and the distribution of these among the kilns of north China.

After the end of the Northern Sung dynasty in 1127–28, when north China fell first to the Chin and then about a century later to the Mongols, the Tz'ŭ-chou type and the closely related black wares seem to have suffered hardly at all; indeed the political changes which elsewhere had somewhat disruptive effects appear rather to have

[1] The earliest instance of black painting on a white slipped body, if this is taken as one of the criteria of the Tz'ŭ-chou type, occurs in the lowest level at Yao-chou, which has been dated late T'ang in the late ninth and tenth centuries. See *Shensi T'ung-ch'üan Yao-chou*, Peking, 1965, p. 16, Plate VII, Figures 13–14.

stimulated in this area new developments and the infusion of new and invigorating ideas in terms of decoration and are also manifested in both the forms and the techniques. One probable reason for this is that both the Tz'ŭ-chou and the black wares had evolved from the start in response to popular demand for purely utilitarian, domestic wares, so that the kilns in effect owed their prosperity to the essential task of satisfying the basic needs of the people around them rather than to the whim of a luxury-loving court set at a distance, and were thus not only unlikely to be affected by changes in the political scene, but were also to be unembarrassed by a withdrawal of imperial patronage, a problem which undoubtedly had to be faced by both the Chün and Ting producing kilns. The fact that the Tz'ŭ-chou and black-ware kilns were in the main dedicated to satisfying domestic requirements meant that from the beginning the products tended to be simple in form and strong in both structure and material, and so they were to remain to the end of their long history; they therefore constitute the most important plebeian wares of the northern regions from at least the beginning of the Northern Sung period onwards until at least the middle of the sixteenth century. In consequence of this common, popular and domestic character both Tz'ŭ-chou and black wares have a robust strength of contour in marked contrast to the refinement, for instance, of Ting, and at the same time little of the sensuous appeal of the best of the Chün or Northern Celadon, whether from Yao-chou or Lin-ju Hsien, the two main production centres of the latter type. For such qualities are substituted freedom, directness and spontaneity of expression, qualities which to some degree are absent from the more sophisticated wares known to have attained imperial favour.

An additional factor contributing to the economic strength of the kilns was almost certainly their wide distribution across the north China plain and farther north into Shansi. In almost every case, so far as we know the locations at present, the kilns were singularly well placed with regard not only to raw materials, but even more important with regard to the lines of communication and access to market centres. From what we know through Ming texts of the region of Hopei particularly the kilns were exceptionally well placed, and even in Ming times the vicinity of Chên-ting Fu was prolific in its production.[1]

The tough durable character of the wares has undoubtedly been a contributory factor to the long survival of the enormous quantity of material. The abundant kiln evidence, which speaks to the value of the wares in the eyes of the Chinese householder, does not make it

[1] *Ta Ming hui-tien* (reprint of Wan-li edition), Vol. 5, Ch. 194, f. 2631b.

clear just how many kilns were active in Yüan times. The sites so far excavated have with one or possibly two exceptions[1] yielded material datable to both the thirteenth and fourteenth centuries. Chinese archaeologists in recent years, however, frankly state that there must still be a great number of sites yet to be identified, and these in addition to those already recorded in the earlier texts, many of which also still have to be identified and located. The archaeologists who worked at Kuan-t'ai and Tz'ŭ-hsien, for example, record that in the region of Hopei alone there are local traditions current over and above those noted in the local history, pointing to a number of kilns which in the future will have to be located and investigated. Even without such archaeological reports as are at present available, it would be possible to follow this varied and important family of wares well into the fourteenth century and beyond, but with the help of the reports we are on firmer ground and it becomes relatively easy to do this and even to distinguish certain local styles.

As to the material itself it is as well to make it clear at once that both the Tz'ŭ-chou type and the black wares are classified as stonewares; that is a pottery fired at temperatures in excess of 1100 degrees centigrade, and are normally covered with a felspathic glaze such as will generally only fuse satisfactorily at about 1200 degrees or more. If glazes that fuse at a lower temperature are used on Tz'ŭ-chou, as does happen when green or turquoise colours derived from copper occur, then the body must be fired first to the high temperature suitable to sinter the stoneware body, after which the coloured glaze can be applied and the piece fired a second time at a lower temperature, one probably not much exceeding 1000 degrees centigrade.[2] Bodies of the Tz'ŭ-chou type particularly display great variations in both colour and texture, variations that are only to be expected in view of the wide distribution of the kilns and the extended period of production. In this respect Tz'ŭ-chou is similar to Chün, but unlike Chün it is relatively rare to find examples with a very dark body. The range of decorative techniques available to the potters is considerable, but all have a common base; in every case the body is dressed with either a slip or a slip-glaze, the latter composed of a higher proportion of clay particles than is normal in glaze. Indeed

[1] Mi-hsien, active in the tenth century, came to an end in the Northern Sung period, and Têng-fêng probably closed in the twelfth century, possibly as early as the Chin invasion.

[2] Lead glazes become volatile at 1050 degrees centigrade, so that the maximum safe temperature is about 1040 centigrade. Alkaline glazes can be fired high, but the Chinese do not seem to have taken the temperature up much farther than the maximum lead temperature at this time for this particular purpose.

without such a base it is unlikely that the decorative effects could be so varied. The glaze applied over either of these bases is either transparent, neutral or coloured, or a dense blackish brown or black, the dark glazes usually being applied over a brown slip-glaze, which has the effect of increasing the density of colour and making possible interesting colour variations in the glaze itself by using reduction firing techniques.

Most of the kilns producing this often spectacular, or by contrast homely group of wares, are concentrated in Hopei, in Tz'ŭ-Hsien (modern Tz'ŭ-chou), Hsiu-wu Hsien, just north of the Yellow river and in the vicinity of Yü-hsien in Honan, while far away to the north in Shansi, not far distant from T'ai-yüan, at Mêng-chia Ching, and at Hung-shan Chên in Chieh-hsiu Hsien was a further group of kilns, which in the Yüan had a rather distinctive style of its own; in addition there was Pa-i in Kao-p'ing Hsien, but the report of this is still awaited. These in the Chin and Yüan seem to have been among the most important, but as already pointed out there must have been many other kilns of which at present nothing is known, If, however, the traditions surviving locally in Hopei are to be relied upon, it would seem that this region will yield a great wealth of material in the future, and that this province together with the large number of kilns in and about Yü-hsien in Honan had the highest output of the types we are at present considering.

It is apparent from the reports so far published that there are certain forms common to all the kilns, and on this basis one might perhaps infer that all of these will occur at those sites which still remain to be discovered. The *mei-p'ing* for instance has been found on all the sites, and we may assume it to have continued in production well beyond the end of the dynasty. Certainly the turquoise glazed ones, which are decoratively organized in the same manner as the southern blue and white ones continued until after the end of the fourteenth century. Into the same category fall the *kuan*, or wine jars, which are likely to have been manufactured at some at least of the same kilns making the *mei-p'ing*, since not only do they often have the same body, but also very often the same organization of the design on the surface, although some of the decorative motifs may differ. Bowls and dishes as well as basins were common currency, though with these forms the decorative techniques were more varied; it seems possible that Yü-hsien in Honan produced some of the more important ranges of these forms. It was also probably here that so many of the large jars with narrow shoulders, small neck and mouth with loop handles at the neck were produced (Plate 93). Head-rests, or pillows, another extremely popular type, seem to have been produced in the greatest quantity by the Chang Company[1] at Tung-ai-k'ou adjacent to Kuan-t'ai in Tz'ŭ-chou; these were of the long rectangular type made as a rule during the Chin and early Yüan (Plate 99A). The recumbent tiger form head-rest was the usual form produced at Yü-hsien (Plate 99B). Thus while there are certain forms common to all kilns, others such as the head-rests, particularly a number of specific forms, seem virtually to have been confined to particular areas. What are still not precisely known are the locations of the kilns producing the almost spherical jars of large size with restricted neck and small mouth of the type represented by the one in the British Museum (Plate 100A) and the one in the Victoria and Albert Museum (Plate 106A), although Yü-hsien suggests itself as a likely area. If we do not know where these were made, nor do we know where the polychrome enamelled bowls, dishes and jars originated, but it is clear from the wide variations in body and in the execution of the decoration, that they were produced at many kilns, one of which was certainly Pa-ts'un in Yü-hsien. It is possible, too, that the loop handled jar decorated in polychrome with bands of flower scroll, birds and animals in the Victoria and Albert Museum (Plate 103A) was made in the Yü-hsien complex,[2] but there is no evidence at present beyond the form which links it to the area. The final form is the pear-shaped vase. There is ample evidence that this was one of the forms in the Yü-hsien repertory, but there must have been other centres besides this which turned out such a popular shape, for it is also found in dark brown and black, some of the specimens with varied glaze effects and others with cut glaze.

In the organization of the decorations, whatever the technique employed, there is during the Yüan a tendency to move away from the freely disposed naturalistic design in favour of a similar naturalism restricted to bands; when the bands are wide they may also be divided up into a series of panels, usually ogival in form, as in the wine jar from Pa-ts'un, and in the cut glaze jar in the Tokyo National Museum (Plates 96A and 106B). The motifs themselves remain predominantly floral with birds, a few animals and sometimes butterflies; the dragon and phoenix make their appearance and children in lotus ponds are not uncommon. To these are added with increasing frequency figure and landscape subjects, the bands of decoration sometimes being separated from each other by abstracted naturalistic elements used as repeats in a scroll, or geometric motifs which include the angular

---

[1] *Wên-wu*, 1964, No. 8, pp. 37–48. The term *chia*, literally house, or family, seems in this context to have meant company, as *chi*, to record, may also mean company in the Kiangsu region.
[2] *Wên-wu*, 1964, No. 8, pp. 27–36.

meander, seen on the Pa-ts'un jar (Plate 96A), formalized scrolling and simple diaper bands of various kinds. Bird and flower motifs frequently attain such a degree of abstraction when used as dominant motifs in the decoration in the black wares that they are often difficult to recognize. A very fine example, less abstract than some, is seen in the ovoid jar painted in black, in Seattle Museum of Art, with its wildly exuberant bird (Plate 93). A more extreme example is one on a similar jar in the Seligman Collection (Plate 94B), which Ayers dates, perhaps with deliberate ambiguity, to 'late Sung'[1] but which, as a northern ware, would more appropriately be assigned to Yüan. The landscape scenes, many of them closely related to the contemporary style of painting among members of the scholar class, are, as might be expected, most commonly found on pillows, which have a conveniently flat surface for painting ornament of this kind; this is the type seen mainly among the pillows produced by the Chang Company, which had its main centre of production at Tung-ai-k'ou near Kuan-t'ai. Finally, inscriptions are often used as decoration, particularly on dishes, which again provide a relatively flat surface suitable for writing single characters, short phrases of a commendatory nature, or even poems; such inscriptions also appear occasionally on wine jars. The dishes on which such inscriptions appear are unfortunately all too often disfigured by the marks of kiln supports, which indicate the common Yüan practice of stacking the dishes one on top of another for firing.[2] Only very rarely are dates inscribed and these are seldom, if ever, part of the main decoration.[3]

BLACK PAINTING ON WHITE SLIP

The application of a white slip to the stoneware body of Tz'ŭ-chou ware served three important purposes: first it acted as a filler if the body were coarse, second it concealed the dismal greyish or brownish body, and third it provided an admirable smooth white surface eminently suitable as a ground for a wide range of visually satisfying decorations carried out in a variety of ways. Painting in dark brown or black slip colour on the white ground must have been one of the earliest methods of decoration, since a few small boxes decorated in this way were found at Yao-chou as early as late T'ang times, or in the tenth century. It became really popular during the Northern

[1] J. Ayers, *Chinese and Korean Pottery and Porcelain* (*Seligman Collection of Oriental Art*, Vol. 2), London, 1964, p. 65, No. D114.

[2] This practice is more apparent in plain white bowls where there is no decoration to camouflage the scars.

[3] The number of dated Tz'ŭ-chou pieces and black wares is very limited, and in most cases the dates are of little help in the dating of other subjects.

Sung period and shared first place among the Tz'ŭ-chou with the *sgraffiato* type. During the thirteenth century it seems to have become much the most common method of decoration on pieces dressed with a white slip. Normally the glaze was a colourless transparent felspathic one, but sometimes it might be slightly opaque, a variation to be accounted for by fluctuations in the firing temperature from one part of the kiln to another and from one firing to another. Any kind of opacity tends to soften and blur the design and generally it is not a common feature, such pieces evidently having been regarded as slightly sub-standard. Painting on the slip was practised at all the kiln sites so far known and was used on almost all forms. In a number of instances the black painted parts have details scratched through them to the white slip beneath, a good representative of this type being one of a large number of deep bowls, often with a small foot, rather swelling body and contracted mouth rim (Plate 94A). The designs on these are characterized by a largeness of scale, even though the decoration lies only on the upper part of the body, neither slip nor glaze reaching more than about two thirds of the way down the outside of the vessel. Such an early example in the period, probably of the earlier part of the thirteenth century, displays a broad treatment with strongly incised lines through the black pigment often accompanied by the use of combing, executed with firm straight strokes. Much later, as in the large wine jar recently excavated in Peking (Plate 95B) it will be noticed that the incising tool is a single point used like a pencil to 'write in' or delineate the details with a fine line. On the evidence we have at present, which is all too little in this respect, it would seem that these came from both Hopei and Honan. The bowl, which is the earlier of the two pieces, may well have come from Kuan-t'ai, but the later wine jar is more likely to have come from Hao-pi-chi in Yü-hsien, Honan, where there seems to have been a practice current of applying a dark glaze to the interior of a jar, instead of a light one as was apparently the habit in Kuan-t'ai.

On dishes, which are open or flat forms, the decoration was generally kept simple, with either a single flower spray confined on the surface by a single line or a multiple series of encircling lines, one of which might be broader than the others. There might also be what Ayers calls a 'bull's eye' in the centre with a highly abstract series of motifs of great simplicity surrounding this and the whole again enclosed within a ring or series of rings (Plate 95A). The practice of writing single characters, four-character phases which were usually auspicious saying or commendations, or even poems appears to have started late in the Northern Sung period, probably with single characters and this continued on into the Yüan with an increase in the use of

111

longer inscriptions in the latter period, the characters always being confined by encircling lines. Neither in form nor in decoration does there appear to have been much change in the course of the Mongol period, the reason perhaps being that such dishes and bowls were mundane objects and not to be regarded as ornamental in their own right.

Vertical forms, however, like jars and vases of various kinds did undergo significant changes. They achieved a more ebullient contour and there was a marked increase in the size of vessel from the beginning of the period to the latter part of the fourteenth century. In every case there is discernible a solid strength, and even if the form as a whole has lost the refined elegance of the early years of Sung development, it has gained in robustness and in the spontaneous, indeed, uninhibited freedom of expression of the potter's taste. On one side one finds the splendid calligraphic freedom of the painter of the Seattle jar (Plate 93), and on the other the studied effects and almost meticulous treatment evidenced by the Pa-ts'un wine jar—if indeed it is a wine jar and not part of a very much larger vessel (Plate 96A). It is possible that it may be the central member of a massive vase like that in Seattle Museum of Art (Plate 97). This astonishing vessel, 88·9 cm. high, has a foot about 30 cm. high, and the long neck spreading to the mouth, the rim of which is turned down in foliations or lapped segments, is just over 30 cm. The body is almost exactly the same shape as the excavated piece, having similar proportions at the neck and base, both of which, even in the photograph, show damage. The organization of the decoration on the body belongs to the same class, even to the subject matter of the ogival panel area. The Seattle vase with its elaborately painted foot and neck clearly belongs to the period, although the first impact one receives is devastating. It is in fact so frankly and flawlessly appalling and so perfect in detail that there can be no doubt as to its authenticity. If Yü-hsien produced it, which seems likely on comparing it with the piece excavated, we can only say we have much to learn about the spontaneous vulgarity of which the Chinese potter, however accomplished technically, was capable. It is worth noting that the true wine jar form differs from these two pieces in having distinctive differences between the diameters of the mouth and the base. It will either be wide at the mouth with a wide rounded shoulder and emphatic taper to the much smaller base, as on the Brundage jar (Plate 96B), with its carelessly painted panels, or it will be noticeably smaller at the mouth than at the base and have more rounded shoulders like the one recently excavated in China with its phoenix bursting out of its enclosing band (Plate 95B). A very much larger jar of monumental proportions and probably intended for storage is in the Chicago Art Institute (Plate 98); it is one of a number of handsome pieces which have been somewhat overlooked in the past. This differs from the wine jars in form, lay-out of design and in the motifs of the decoration, but belongs to the same fourteenth-century tradition. It is painted with the flowers of the four seasons in lobed panels on the flattened shoulder and it should be remarked that as in the Peking wine jar, there is a casual disregard for the band within which the design is conceptually organized. The same tendency may be seen on the large almost spherical bottle formerly in the Oppenheim Collection (Plate 100A), a piece which like the Chicago jar has an undulating line in one band of the decoration. Similar in shape and equally fluent in decoration is the larger bottle in Plate 100B. The unusual lotus scroll reserved against a hatched wave ground on the shoulders is separated from the long poetic inscription below by a narrow chevron border of leaves and florets. The spontaneous painting of this impressive group with its disregard of margin limitations is quite unlike that of either the Pa-ts'un jar, Seattle vase or the globular bottle in the Brundage Collection, which all have the segmented wave hatched background to at least a part of the decoration, and in every case a strict regard for the limitations imposed by the margins. These two groups may be separated to some extent in time and space, but they both clearly belong to the same artistic climate in which boldness and strength have an important part to play.

The two main types of pillows with painted designs in black on white slip have already been mentioned. The rectangular pillows made by the Chang Company at Tung-ai-k'ou, which usually bear impressed marks, of which the most common is *Chang-chia ts'ao*, are generally decorated on the top surface with landscapes in a rather delicate style not found elsewhere in the Tz'ŭ-chou painted wares (Plate 99A). When landscapes are not used, as in the side panels or even occasionally on the top surface, the style is bolder and closer to other wares of this group. The spandrels filling the area between the panels and the outer border of meander are embellished with floral designs, often of a rather fussy character, the flower most popularly used being the pomegranate. The second type of pillow in the form of a recumbent tiger is painted in a much broader style (Plate 99B). The black is less dense in tone, often indeed being a deep brown, and is sometimes supplemented by a very pale brown which the Chinese refer to in their archaeological reports as 'red', but which could better be described as a soft pinkish brown. The slip ground of the recumbent tiger pillows is usually rather a creamy tone and the glaze is thin and slightly less glossy than that used on the rectangular pillows.

YÜAN PORCELAIN AND STONEWARE

During the earlier period under the Sung and Chin a transparent green lead glaze was sometimes used on painted pieces, but this seems to have been abandoned during Mongol times in favour of a brilliant turquoise blue, possibly an introduction from the Islamic west, where the colour had long been in use, and which fitted in well with the splendours of the new artistic taste. The use of this colour was of long standing in Iran and farther west at Raqqa in Mesopotamia and since following the Mongol invasions the way was open for transmission not only of goods but of ideas by merchants, it seems possible that the appearance of turquoise was a consequence of renewed contact with the Near East. What is now important to notice is that while the colourless transparent glaze on Chinese stoneware at this time is always felspathic, the turquoise glaze is alkaline, being fluxed with soda/lime constituents rather than with the high potash content as in the case of the Chinese felspathic glaze; and it is not fluxed with lead, because with the copper as a colourant this would only produce the familiar green of earlier times. In order to gain turquoise instead of green it is essential to use a glaze in which lead has been reduced to a minumum and preferably is not present at all.[1] Alkaline glaze has one fault in common with lead glaze, which has probably led to the mistaken belief that both the turquoise and the green are lead glazes: it is that both are subject to decay in very similar ways, and it is rare to find a turquoise piece entirely free of crazing. It is possible that in the Yüan period, particularly in the earlier years, the green lead glaze was still being used, but it is fairly clear from both the forms and the decorative styles that at least by the fourteenth century the alkaline turquoise glaze had completely ousted the green in popular favour; the fact is particularly noted in the archaeological report on Hao-po-chi in Yü-hsien.[2] Both glazes fire at a lower temperature than stoneware, so that pieces on which these colours appear are always biscuit fired, a procedure not essential for the colourless felspathic type. The forms are mainly *kuan* type wine jars and *mei-p'ing*, although a small number of bowls with small foot, low swelling sides and inverted rim as well as round boxes are recorded. The wine jars are frequently decorated with dragons and phoenix round the middle and lower part, with a band of floral scroll, cursively executed round the shoulder against a cross-hatched ground. The main band of decoration is large in scale and dynamically drawn against a scrolling cloud-filled ground as is iconographically fitting for these two motifs. The *mei-p'ing* on the other hand is more fussily treated with somewhat stylized flower

[1] C. W. Parmelee, *Ceramic glazes*, 1951, pp. 218–219, 'Blue' and 'Green'. See also D. Rhodes, *Clay and glazes for the potter*, 1963, p. 130.

[2] *Wên-wu*, 1964, No. 8, pp. 1–14.

scrolls, smaller in scale and set out in a series of bands, usually three, separated from each other by triple encircling lines, the middle one of which is wider than the others, or by a band of angular meander as on the vase in the Victoria and Albert Museum (Colour Plate G). The form is rather heavy, with a small neck, rather square shoulder and only a slight taper towards the flanged base; this is a good and fairly typical example, especially in the treatment of the base, though in many instances the somewhat fluid glaze runs down over the projecting ridge at the bottom. There are some examples in which the main band of decoration consists of a series of lobed panels enclosing landscape scenes, sometimes with figures as well, but the floral scroll as a shoulder element seems invariable. The background against which floral scrolls are painted is always either simply hatched, or hatched with something like the segmented wave pattern. On the small bowls the same treatment is to be seen with the same handling of the background. Both *mei-p'ing* and bowls have a compact fine-grained brownish stoneware body quite unlike the *kuan* wine jars, which have a coarse grey body, an indication, even apart from the style, of a different centre of production, and one which may well have continued into the Ming dynasty, when turquoise glazed *mei-p'ing* were not uncommon. The likelihood is that these were later in being introduced and may have been part of the production from Chên-ting-fu area in Hopei, which was well known in Ming times for its large output.[1]

POLYCHROME ENAMELLED DECORATION

No satisfactory explanation has so far been proposed for the unheralded appearance of overglaze polychrome decoration on the Tz'ŭ-chou wares. The only fact we can be sure of is that it occurs about the end of the twelfth century, the earliest dated example being a bowl in the Tokyo National Museum dated to 1201, that is in the last years of the Chin (Plate 101A). The popularity of the type must have increased rapidly, and although so far the only site to yield fragments has been Pa-ts'un, the wide variations in bodies through innumerable examples of bowls of the same size and shape, with closely similar decoration, indicates clearly the wide distribution of the technique and the universal acceptance of the decorative style. The bowls, the most common form, are rounded with a straight mouth rim and a neatly cut foot-ring; the shallow dishes of very similar diameter are probably the next most common shape. The body, whatever the shape, is dressed with an evenly applied white slip

[1] *Ta Ming hui-tien*, Ch. 194, f. 2631a and b.

inside and down about two thirds of the outside, and the same area is covered by the glaze; the glaze rarely extends beyond the limit of the slip on the outside. The only class on which the slip and glaze totally cover the body, foot, base and all, consists of small hemispherical bowls, rather thin in the body and with only a vestigial foot-ring of small diameter. They are the only type of bowl, some little larger than egg-cups, to be decorated on the outside, the design invariably being of lotus petals. This family has only begun to appear on the market in recent years and some are so brilliant in glaze and without trace of wear such as one normally finds on enamelled wares, or of traces of burial, that perhaps one may be pardoned for entertaining doubts as to their authenticity. In other respects, that is the decoration of the inside, these bowls adhere to the same general rule as all other pieces of bowl or dish form. The designs are retained in the central area by a series of rings in red, sometimes lobed, either three or four of equal thinness, or with one of them thicker than the others (Plate 101B); as in early pieces, the design is large in scale, generally consisting of a flower spray freely disposed to fill the space, the peony and lotus being the flowers most favoured; occasionally the mallow combines with the peony. If purely floral decorations are not used, then birds or fish are introduced against a background of lotus; in a few cases single characters, or four characters, are organized in the central field. Whatever the motif the scale continues to be large until about the middle of the fourteenth century on all forms. The dated bowl in Tokyo which would seem to belong to the earliest series, is unusual in having the red floral decoration of the central field set against a green ground. There are not many examples of this kind, but another good one with added yellow dots on the wide red ring encircling the central element is in the Art Institute in Chicago. Whether or not this type represents an early stage or indicates some local style still remains to be discovered. The more usual treatment is to leave the central decoration silhouetted on the white or slightly cream coloured ground. The scale of the main decoration within the limit allotted to it began gradually to diminish, a part of the method of achieving this being to enlarge the area by reducing the width of the encircling lines and pushing them outwards nearer the rim; the number of elements in the central field were then sometimes increased, or they were slightly elaborated, lotus flowers and leaves for instance acquiring stems and scrolling elements that acted as fillers. The Detroit bowl (Plate 101c), the largest so far recorded, with a duck swimming in a lotus pond with additional water-weed, is probably the best example of the change. A final point should be remarked about these bowls and dishes; from the earliest stage onward the pieces were evidently

G. *Turquoise* mei-p'ing *vase with painting in black. Ht. 26·7 cm.*
Victoria and Albert Museum

stacked one on top of another in the first high temperature firing, for the inside surface is marred by five spur marks. Fortunately the potters soon appreciated this fault and in later examples the defect is reduced to a minimum, but even the Detroit bowl is disfigured in this way, and not even the carefully calculated application of enamels wholly camouflages it.

The variety of forms so far recorded for this type is somewhat limited but doubtless as excavations are carried out and new material is identified it may be possible to redate many pieces and take a firmer grasp on unfamiliar forms, which because of their peculiarities instil in us doubts as to their authenticity. There are, however, familiar forms such as stem-cups, deep bowls with almost vertical sides and pear-shaped vases, the latter being perhaps more familiar among the Yüan pieces in the black painted type. The pear-shaped vases in polychrome are generally small, rarely being more than about 20 cm. high; the form is rather slack-looking, the foot being rather wide and the neck insufficiently narrow for elegance, a quality more usually seen on the larger black painted or cut glazed types. The decoration round the outside of the deep bowls and on the vases is organized in a wide band, or a series of small bands of naturalistic and formal designs, the use of several bands being the more usual treatment of the vases. On the basis of form it would seem that the vases come mainly from Pa-ts'un and the vicinity of Yü-hsien, where the black painted variety having similar proportions and displaying a like distribution of motifs on the surface were found and were illustrated in the report published in 1964.

Another form, already familiar in the black painted type and again recorded among the Pa-ts'un finds, is the ovoid jar with two or four loop handles at the junction of the narrow neck and shoulder. The best example in polychrome is probably that in the Victoria and Albert Museum (Plate 103A), which has hitherto been attributed to the Ming dynasty. In view of the trilobate elements on the shoulder it would probably be correct to assign this to the fourteenth century, an attribution which gains support from the dark glazed band at the neck and the fact that both slip and glaze stop quite tidily about 2·5 cm. or so above the neatly cut slightly spreading foot-ring. The uninhibited character of the two bands of decoration accord well with a fourteenth-century date, but because of the introduction of an overglaze brown on this particular specimen, it should perhaps be placed in the second half of the century. The use of an overglaze brownish enamel is repeated in the decoration of a number of *kuan* which continue well into the Ming dynasty. The *kuan* form does not appear to have been included in the repertory so far recorded for the Hopei sites, so that it seems likely that at least some of the larger examples, which we know, may well have come from the more central Honan sites. Two good examples of *kuan*, with their carefully painted genre and landscape scenes, were shown in the Yüan exhibition in Cleveland in 1968. Stylistically, both in the proportions they display and in the division of surface, the polychrome examples are close to the black painted ones. Of the two the St. Louis specimen is the simpler, the Metropolitan Museum one being greatly enriched by the elaboration of the shoulder decoration, which includes petal band and a floral scroll together with a formal scrolling pattern round the neck (Plate 103B). The floral scroll round the shoulder relates this piece to the black painted jars with either colourless or turquoise glaze, of which the one shown in Colour Plate G is an example. This type of wine jar continued through the end of Yüan and well into the Ming, the latest example of the type being one inscribed with a date equivalent to 1541.[1] The tendency in form was for the lower part of the vessel to become so elongated as time passed that the exaggeration forced the potters to give the base a spread like that on the vase in the Tokyo National Museum, one which may well date into the earliest years of the Ming. Ultimately the form was abandoned, but not before the exaggerated elongation had reached the point of absurdity.

One other group of polychrome enamelled ware needs to be mentioned. This consists of a series of small figures of men, women and children, all of them made in moulds with little attempt at detailed modelling. Whether these were originally intended as toys, as seems possible, or were simply popular ornamental objects, is not clear. There is a considerable number of them and a fragment of one was found at Pa-ts'un, so some at least were made there, but they were probably produced at other centres as well. The figures vary in size from about 15 to 25 cm. high and are gaily painted in red, green and yellow, and with a dense black for the details of the features and the hair, together with occasional details in other parts (Plates 102A, B). The group is of interest for two reasons: first the painting of the robes reflects the textile patterns of the time, mainly of the thirteenth and fourteenth centuries, and second, because these figures may have sparked off the manufacture in Islam of a somewhat similar series of small figures on which the glaze was often transparent turquoise, a highly favoured colour in the Near East. This is perhaps less unlikely than one might think, since as popular ware such objects would certainly be on sale in most of the local markets and thus be seen by foreign merchants in north China, who might well buy these delightful, easily portable souvenirs to take home across central Asia,

[1] This jar was in the Thiel Collection in Los Angeles.

when they returned with their more usual merchandise, which was likely to be silk piece-goods.

SGRAFFIATO AND CUT GLAZE

One of the earliest techniques in Tz'ŭ-chou ware was that of *sgraffiato*, which in its inspiration was dependent upon metalworking.[1] The incised lines cut through a white slip for the main outlines of the decoration imitating the traced line in silver, the design then being thrown up in emphasis by filling the background with small rings also imitating precisely the ring-matted ground in silverworking, was undoubtedly laborious and the potters even in Sung times had begun to move towards quicker methods of achieving the effects they needed. The ring-matted ground gave way either to a striated ground or was cut away completely to the body which gave an even more prominent place to the decorative elements. By the thirteenth century the ring-matted ground had probably been completely abandoned and the large bowls, basins and jars that can be attributed to Yüan are either striated or have the ground cut away. Bowls and basins decorated in the *sgraffiato* technique always have a striated ground, since to cut the slip right away would have been unsuitable aesthetically and practically for such objects. The main lines of the designs were sketched rather briskly and were often stiff, as for instance may be seen on the Mount Trust bowl (Plate 104A) and the basin with flattened rim in the Tokyo National Museum (Plate 104B). By the fourteenth century it is possible that even this treatment had been given up as being too laborious, painting being much quicker to carry out on a slipped body. On vases and jars the practice of cutting the slip away to the body continued, but examples with white slip under a colourless glaze are not common in the fourteenth century and in style they are very different from those in the earlier tradition. Two characteristic specimens of the late style, however, are the rather large pear-shaped vase shown in the exhibition in Tokyo in 1970, datable to the period 1314–1324 (Plate 105A), and a large wine jar, which was once in the Eumorfopoulos Collection (Plate 105B). Both are decorated with bands of petal panels and birds among flower scrolls. The treatment of the surface in a series of unrelated elements juxtaposed in a succession of bands is one of the most characteristic

---

[1] The suggestion put forward by Ayers in the *Seligman Catalogue*, that the *sgraffiato* technique was evolved in an attempt to imitate carved Ting is not borne out by the facts. It clearly derived directly from metalworking as indicated by the finds from Mi-hsien, the products of which antedate carved Ting. The suggestion was, however, made prior to the publication of the Mi-hsien report in *Wên-wu* in 1964, No. 8.

features of the period. The only other example of this type, and one on which apart from the stylistic features the dating of these depends, is the wine jar, very similar to the Eumorfopoulos one, which was found in excavations on a Yüan site at Chi-ning-lu in Inner Mongolia.[1] It was found in association with two black painted pieces with white ground, one of which was certainly Yüan, and with some black and brown glazed jars small at the neck and having the loop handles common to the type as represented by the Seattle jar. There is no indication at the moment as to where these rather splendid, if rare, pieces were made and there do not seem to be any parallels among the cut-glazed type, which is a variant form of *sgraffiato*.

The cut-glazed family is the boldest and most spectacular of the Tz'ǔ-chou in the Yüan period. The very hard buff or pale grey body is almost invariably covered with a thick viscous dark brown to black slip glaze, which while still damp is cut away in bold, large-scale designs. These may be floral, but scrolling leaf patterns and angular meanders are more common; often details are incised, and occasionally the whole design is incised as it is in the case of the almost spherical jar with a band of fish and lotus in water in the Victoria and Albert Museum (Plate 106A). Fortunately the group can be approximately dated from the similarly shaped incised jar with a boy sporting among foliage in the British Museum which is dated to 1305.[2] Most pieces are boldly conceived in form with simple well-defined contours, and the decoration is fluent, strong, and executed with almost unparalleled assurance. The large wine jars, with the glaze properly cut away, as opposed to the incised type, are usually found to have the main band of decoration ordered in ogival panels, as on the handsome example in Tokyo National Museum (Plate 106B), but on smaller pieces and on the pear-shaped vases the decoration generally flows in one or more unbroken bands round the body as on the St. Louis vase (Plate 107). The type probably continued to the end of the fourteenth century, the later examples becoming more fussy and less striking in their visual impact.

A variant group of this family comes from one of the kilns in Shansi.[3] This is characterized by ogival panels, with rather more extensive cutting of the glaze in this area, and by scoring the rest of

[1] *Wên-wu*, 1961, No. 9, p. 52. A coloured illustration of the jar is included in *Nei-mêng-ku ch'u-t'u wên-wu hsüan-chi*, Peking, 1963, Plate 169.

[2] J. Ayers, 'Some characteristic wares of the Yüan period', *T.O.C.S.* 1954, Plate 44, fig. 38.

[3] The type is traditionally associated with the province and most of the excavated material has been found here and to the north in Inner Mongolia. It is possible that the report on the work at Pa-i, which has yet to be published, may prove helpful.

the ground, often in a segmented wave patterning (Plate 108A). In this group the *mei-p'ing* makes its appearance, an early, probably thirteenth-century example being the one in the Seligman Collection with its truncated conical mouth and rather narrow sloping shoulders. Later the form changed with the shoulder becoming straight with a fairly sharp angular turn downward to the foot. There are also some handsome deep bowls with well-rounded body and neatly cut slightly spreading foot-ring. The body of the type is hard, not particularly fine-grained, and greyish, being somewhat speckled with light brown ferruginous particles. The glaze is generally less glossy than that of the Honan black glazed type, and it is also rather more carelessly applied, little trouble being taken to ensure neatness round the lower limit.

BLACK GLAZED WARES

There are a number of easily distinguished groups of black and dark brown glazed stonewares in addition to the cut-glazed type, which continue and elaborate a tradition going back into the Northern Sung period, when most of the pieces were relatively much smaller than was to be usual in Yüan times. The pale buff, greyish, or more rarely white stoneware body is generally covered with a slip glaze of dark brownish tone and a second darker glaze is applied over this. Not only does the technique produce a very dense colour if this is desired, but it also makes possible interesting painted and splashed effects, usually in bright rusty brown, but sometimes in steel blue-black, produced by reduction firing. Contrary to the general belief most of the northern black glazed stonewares are subjected to reduction at some stage in the firing.

Rust brown speckling, splashing and painting is characteristic of the group, the colour being achieved by applying an iron oxide to the slip glaze before the application of the second glaze. Normally even in reducing conditions 10 per cent or more of iron oxide will produce a dense lustrous black in a felspathic glaze, but between 3 and 5 per cent applied to a really viscous glaze and given strong reducing conditions towards the end of the firing will result in a rusty metallic brown similar to the attractive effects achieved on the northern wares. Sometimes the colour balancing is reversed so that the patterning appears dark blue-black against a brownish black ground. Brown spotted and streaked vases and jars have both been found at Kuan-t'ai in Tz'ŭ-hsien, but in a fragmentary state so are not easy to date, but we are informed that the pieces were sturdily constructed, and that the glaze on the outside did not generally reach the foot, which is often an indication of Yüan, or at least thirteenth-century date.

Pear-shaped vases with highly abstract paintings of birds in flight or of leaf sprays in brown on black or in blue-black against a deep brownish ground are fairly common judging by the number of examples surviving to the present day; one of the best of this type is the one formerly in the Oppenheim Collection (Plate 109A). The same motif may also occur on the broad shouldered wine jar of *kuan* type, of which there is an example in the Barlow Collection dating perhaps a little earlier than the former Oppenheim piece. On these vases and on the jars, as well as on the immense jars with small neck, like the one shown in Tokyo in 1970, the glaze reaches right down to the foot, and although the foot-ring itself is bare of glaze, there is often a rough application on the base and round the inner wall of the foot-ring. The most magnificent of the type is the massive, indeed monumental jar shown in Tokyo (Colour Plate H). Painted in a warm rust brown with a metallic lustre against a dense blackish glaze with peony sprays and rather cursive butterflies, it represents a peak in this class of production in north China in the late thirteenth and fourteenth centuries. The base glaze on this is a thin watery brown, while the main glaze is thick and dense, but however thick and dense, it neither conceals the lines left by the potter's hands as he threw the vessel on the wheel, nor does it hide the fact that the jar was constructed in two main parts placed one on top of the other, the junction being just discernible on the line running round at the base of the flower and along the leaf stem to the left. Where this massive jar was made is not known, but Honan would seem a likely area. Bowls of great simplicity are also found in this group, some of them of exceptionally large size. They are plain black on the outside, the brown painting on the inside consisting of simple stripes radiating from the centre. Like many of the thirteenth- and fourteenth-century production they are stoutly constructed and often well finished, although it is not uncommon, among the bowls at least, for the glaze to run down to form a thick welt on the outside and to pool in the inside, or to gather in treacly globules. Whether the bowls were made in Hopei or Honan is not yet known, but there is evidence concerning the origin of another group, different in character, which certainly came from Honan, though other areas may have produced similar material of which we as yet know nothing. The pieces forming the group are often massive, with white ribs in relief against a glossy black (Plate 109B). They were made at Pa-ts'un and also at other kilns in the area; the region seems to have been especially prolific in high quality material. The repertory of form includes a small number of ewers of somewhat unusual shape having a stocky cylindrical body, rounded shoulder and long narrow cylindrical neck, with a loop handle from the neck to the base of the shoulder, from which a curving spout rises on the opposite side. There are also jars and vases of forms similar to those already described in connection with other decorative techniques. Many small jars, which are probably early in date, perhaps as early as Northern Sung, were succeeded in Yüan by very much larger ones, many of which, unlike the earlier ones, are only partly glazed on the outside and on which the glaze does not always reach right down and across the bottom inside. The bodies were either coarse-grained, but well-compacted and hard pale buff, or were extremely fine-grained, very hard and almost white, clearly indicating that more than one kiln was involved in the manufacture of the type. In actual fact there seem to have been at least three centres involved, Pa-ts'un, Hao-pi-chi and Tuan-tien, all in Honan. Examination of this variant group suggests that the base glaze was a thick very dark one on which the white ribs were trailed as a stiff slip to form the ribs, the whole then being covered with a transparent colourless glaze, which in firing became slightly contaminated by the darker underlying glaze. The technical accomplishment of this succession of operations required considerable skill and a nice judgement of glaze composition and consistency, as well as very precise timing in making the successive applications.

In closing any discussion of Tz'ŭ-chou type pottery it might seem unnecessary to stress the importance of technical advances in glaze handling and in firing techniques, yet it is perhaps as well to do so because Tz'ŭ-chou and its related black ware is one of the least understood of all the potteries the Chinese produced. This may very largely be due to the fact that it did not at any time, apparently, achieve imperial recognition. Perhaps in view of the Chinese connoisseur's capacity, or lack of it, to understand the techniques it was as well, for there is less nonsense written in Chinese antiquarian handbooks about Tz'ŭ-chou than any of the others, and in some works it does not even get a mention. In the future we can start with a clean sheet and an open mind about the material and we shall hope that future excavation will reveal at least where all these different types were made, as well perhaps as to provide a basis for a really sound chronology from late T'ang to Ming.

7

CHI-CHOU AND THE
MINOR SOUTHERN KILNS

The prefectural city of Chi-chou lies about two hundred and fifty kilometres south of Jao-chou in Kiangsi, and has given its name to a varied range of pottery produced at the kilns located eight kilometres to the north at Yung-ho on the west bank of the Kan river. Prior to the Yüan this group of kilns was of major importance in the province and one which was accorded the status of being 'semi-official', in as much as there was an official posted there to oversee the government taxation in respect of the pottery production and the commercial transactions. The products of the kilns are variously known by the names Kian, Chi-an and Chian, the most nearly correct name being Chi-an, which was the original name of Chi-chou in Han times. The name Chi-chou, implying prefectural status, was awarded in the Five Dynasties period, retained throughout Sung, but in Yüan it was renamed Chi-an, or more properly Chi-an Lu, Lu being an administrative unit; Yung-ho itself was a Chên or market town within the administrative area comprehended by Chi-an Lu. In all the modern texts relating to the products of Yung-ho, the Chinese use the name Chi-chou and it is therefore appropriate to prefer and use this name here.

The kilns, situated as they were on the west bank of the Kan river, were well placed for the distribution of their products, which could be carried north down the river to Nan-chang and thence to the same distribution centres as were to be used by Jao-chou, the kiln area to supersede Chi-chou in the fourteenth century. The products could also be sent southwards up the river and by a simple porterage over the watershed between the head of the Kan river and the turn of the Peh river through the Mei-ling Pass; the goods reverted to water transport at Shiu-chou for passage down to Canton, which in Sung times was still a flourishing port handling the bulk of the export trade, and which continued to have importance, though gradually diminishing in the Yüan period. It was probably through this port that most of the Chi-chou material found abroad passed during the Sung period, especially that destined for Indonesia. The sites of waster and refuse heaps cover a considerable area and indicate a large output over a prolonged period. Brankston visited the region and made known some of the products in 1938,[1] but it was not until about 1953 that the Chinese began any serious investigation. Even this, however, did not amount to more than a general survey.[2] The report of this, published in 1958,[3] suggests that the extensive disturbance which has occurred in the course of the passing centuries is far greater than would have been caused only by farmers clearing land for cultivation and that it might also be accounted for in part by some massive natural disaster. The upheaval has made close dating of the material almost impossible. The report states, however, that the period of greatest activity is likely to have been from the tenth to the end of the twelfth century, after which a slow decline began, with craftsmen beginning a steady drift northwards to Jao-chou, especially during the Yüan, when the sharp increase in output and new concentration on porcelain constituted an economic attraction and resulted in the cessation of Chi-chou in the early days of the Ming. The hypothetical natural disaster already mentioned may well have been a factor serving to hasten the decline. There have not so far been any discoveries of actual kilns and it is not precisely known how many were in fact established there, although the *Ching-tê Chên T'ao-lu*, a somewhat unreliable source, states that there were five at one time.[4] All the Chinese team discovered out of the twenty-odd waster heaps was one, Number 12, on which there was a vast amount of kiln furniture, which included saggars, firing stands and quantities of iron tools; there were similar finds on some of the other heaps but none so numerous. Another difficulty which has made valid inference from the sites impossible is that many of the heaps appear to have been man-made, by farmers clearing fields for cultivation. Thus until a series of systematic excavations are undertaken we are thrown back on style in any study of the material.

In actual description of finds and of the main types, Jan Wirgin's

---

[1] A. D. Brankston, 'An excursion to Ching-te-chen and Chi-an-fu in Kiangsi', *T.O.C.S.*, Vol. 16, 1938–39, pp. 19–32.

[2] The preliminary report was published under the title *Chi-chou yao i chih kai-kuang* in *Wên-wu ts'an-k'ao Tzŭ-liao*, 1953, No. 9, p. 88.

[3] *Chi-chou yao*, Ch'iang Hsüan-t'ai, Peking, 1958.

[4] G. R. Sayer's translation, London, 1951, p. 63. It should be noted that this is even in Chinese a late source dating from 1815 and consequently somewhat unreliable.

paper 'Some ceramic wares of Chi-chou',[1] is a valuable starting point, based as it is to a large extent on the Chinese reports of 1953 and 1958, but the problems of dating were necessarily only briefly alluded to, although certain helpful aspects of the relationship between Chi-chou and Lung-ch'üan and Ching-tê Chên were discussed.

The best known types produced in Sung times at least were the so-called leaf *temmoku* (Plate 110A) and the bowls with paper-cut decorations (Plate 110B), and it is probably fair to assume that both of these continued in production well into the Yüan. Of the two it is likely that the paper-cut type persisted longer. The bowl shapes were fairly standard, being either simple conical or rounded with either a straight or a restricted rim, while the foot-ring was usually rather carelessly cut, and not uncommonly appears vestigial. The leaf-decorated type generally has a reddish buff body, or it may be slightly gingery, and is coarse grained. The paper-cut ones have a similarly coarse body, but they are grey, sometimes quite a dark grey. Both types are fully glazed down to the foot, the paper-cut ones with a tortoise-shell dark brown and yellowish mottling on the outside (Plate 110C). The difference in body colour is one resulting from the firing cycle used and not to any fundamental difference in the material of the body. The leaf *temmoku* were fired in an oxidizing atmosphere and thus the body becomes light brownish, while the paper-cut bowls were fired in a reducing atmosphere which invariably produces a grey body when the clay is a noticeably heavy iron-bearing one. The method of applying the decoration was probably the same in both cases, the leaf or paper-cut being attached to the raw body with a light adhesive of some kind and the glaze then being added over it.[2] In the firing the pattern emerges from the natural constituents of the material in the firing reaction. The paper-cuts, appearing black against a mottled or streaked ground, include simple repeats of prunus flowers, carefully placed floral medallions, flower or fruit sprays, birds and butterflies, and finally four-character phrases in cusped panels, most of them conveying popular phrases of good luck of a common kind, such as *Ch'ang-ming fu-kuei*, 'Long life, wealth and honour', or *Fu-shou k'ang-ning*, 'Wealth, longevity, health and peace'. The popularity of these paper-cut bowls must have been enormous, for very large numbers of them are known, many of them in a good state of preservation. The precise dating must obviously

---

[1] *Bulletin of the Museum of Far Eastern Antiquities*, No. 34, Stockholm, 1962.

[2] Technically there is no necessity for yellowish painting on the place where the leaf was to rest in the leaf *temmoku* type as the report suggests and apparently accepted by Wirgin. The glaze reaction during the firing cycle adopted is sufficient to account for the final result.

remain problematical as there have been relatively few finds of Chi-chou material in tombs despite the known wide distribution of the wares proved by the recovery of sherds from a great number of different parts of south China.

Also occurring at Chi-chou are two groups of stonewares with seemingly cut-glaze decoration, one using a black glaze and the other a white or neutral glaze. How far the appearance of the decoration is due to the influence of Tz'ŭ-chou in the north is an open question, but in view of the extreme divergence in the decorative style it seems more likely to have been an independent development; the designs have nothing whatever in common with Tz'ŭ-chou, the whole conception of surface being quite different. Besides this the originality of the Chi-chou potter, already demonstrated in the leaf *temmoku* and the paper-cut type, is again displayed here in the complete understanding of the ceramic materials of both body and glaze, the decorative techniques used in these two being unique to Chi-chou. Of the two groups the neutral glazed type, on a very pale buff stoneware or whitish porcellanous body of rather thin construction, was the earlier. It probably began in the Southern Sung period, as indicated by the find of two pieces in a possible Southern Sung tomb near Nanking, but continued into Yüan.[1] In this group are found round boxes with low-domed lids and small jars with wide overlapping domed lid, sometimes with undulating rims of the kind that could be described, as Gray so aptly does in another connexion, as 'pastry work'. The most popular decoration of this type of box and jar was apparently a prunus spray, usually with a crescent moon, a design which remained popular in Yüan and is found also on the Lung-ch'üan celadons. The design is almost always organized in the same way, with the blossoms on the main, more or less straight stem with added leaves, and further leaves and a bud on a second stem, which forks away to one side and is then sharply angled back, often across the main stem. The potters seem to have used two different methods of executing this design on the white wares. Either they could lay a stencil down on the still slightly damp body, cut a few lines into the body through the open sections and then paint with a resist, and finally after removing the stencil cover the whole with glaze, as seems to have been done on the Bernat box (Plates 111B, C), or a paper cut-out could be lightly stuck to the surface with an adhesive, the glaze applied and the cut-out immediately removed, as in the case of the Bristol vase (Plate 111A). The

[1] See *K'ao-ku*, 1958, No. 12, p. 35, a brief report by Ch'ên Wan-li. The evidence for a Southern Sung date appears flimsy but not impossible; it is based on numismatic evidence ensuring a date not earlier than 1200 but it could be a century or even more later.

distinction between the two techniques is a fine one, only the breaks in the pattern indicating when a stencil was most likely used. When the paper cut-out was removed it was still possible to incise details and this clearly shows on the Bristol vase. It will be noticed that the glaze on these white pieces, while forming an adequate protective coating, is rather less durable than on other wares. It seems to be softer, less well fitting and subject to decay. It is nearly always cracked and on edges and along angular contours tends to break away, while the body has a dry almost sugary texture, especially on those with the least good glaze fit.

Such faults do not occur on the black glazed type, in which not only are the dominant forms different, but also the decorations, which tend to be much more varied, although the prunus spray is still fairly frequently seen. An interesting difference between the white glazed type and the black glazed type is that in the black glazed type the details are not incised but painted in quite neatly in dark brown, as on the Barlow vase (Plate 112A). The design is always executed using a paper-cut which is peeled off the surface while the body and glaze are still damp, the colour is then applied and sometimes a little of the body cut away as well to give emphasis to the main lines of the decoration. The proof of the use of paper-cuts being stuck on to the body and then peeled off while both body and glaze are damp is to be seen in the *mei-p'ing* from the St. Louis City Art Museum (Plate 112B). Not only does the body, where this is exposed, show the rilling lines occurring in the throwing process, but at the tip of one petal of every flower there is a slight nick in the body and edge of the glaze where the craftsman has lifted the paper-cut out with his finger nail or with a sharp instrument. One of the florets towards the bottom is badly messed up owing to the craftsman removing the paper-cut too quickly after the glaze had been applied; one or two of the ellipsoid stamen elements also show slight smudging that has occurred as the pattern was removed. The technique lends itself to one delightful variant, a representative of which is a vase in the Victoria and Albert Museum. This is to use a real leaf or frond of fern and peel it away in the same manner. In this particular example the glaze is a pale one, but it is possible that a dark glaze may also have been used.

The most important group of Chi-chou wares attributed to Yüan are the dark brown painted type, the colour being applied to a pale cream slipped body of extremely fine-grained dense pale buff clay, and the whole covered with a thin transparent glaze. This is much the most varied group in both form and decoration. It included small rotund jars (Plates 113A, B), some with lugs on the shoulder, pear-shaped vases, tripods (of which none are illustrated in the Chinese report), a few ewers and possibly some plates or dishes, fragments of these forms having been found on the waster heaps, and finally some large vases, either roughly pear-shaped (Plate 114), or of rather curious ungainly form quite unlike any represented in other wares (Plate 115). In the decorative motifs, however, they are in some respects closely related to the blue and white of Jao-chou, especially in the persistent use of the wave pattern and a version of the knobbed scroll, the latter being a distinctive Mongol element, as pointed out by Ayers.[1] Both these elements are normally kept for background use, but occasionally they become a major theme. Against such backgrounds the painters placed heavily outlined panels which are always lobed and which enclose naturalistic motifs such as flower sprays or animals, often drawn with a brisk cursive dash. The use of lobed panels is, of course, a common feature in Tz'ŭ-chou ware, but the northern type is always ogival while those of Chi-chou are the bow-lobed variety, quite distinct from the ogival kind, and seem to be an independent development of the Chi-chou potters, who were clearly both inventive and skilful. The decorations used are, apart from the birds and flower sprays in the panels, frequently adapted from other media. The knobbed scroll for instance is drawn from textiles, almost certainly the Mongol type stitched felts, while the diaper bands round the neck of the very unusual jar in Plate 115 are most likely taken over from a woven brocaded textile. The body decoration of this piece and the somewhat similar design on the neck of the British Museum's massive vase is adapted from silk embroidery. There are other sources, too, from which designs were adopted. The band at the base of the neck below the two moulded fish handles on the British Museum vase with its interlacing pattern is evidently taken over from basketry or wickerwork. It is a type of patterning also found in a slightly modified form on late fourteenth- and early fifteenth-century Lung-ch'üan celadons. The narrow angular meander at the mouth rim on the same piece is a well-known motif, the immediate antecedent source being metalwork, but ultimately stemming from stone carving.[2] The wave patterns on all the painted pieces are so closely affiliated to those current in the blue and white farther north that it has been suggested, no more than speculatively, that Chi-chou may have exerted an influence on Ching-tê Chên rather than the other way about.[3] Without the evidence of much dated and closely datable material, however,

[1] J. Ayers, 'Some characteristic wares of the Yüan dynasty', *T.O.C.S.*, 29, 1954–55, p. 85.

[2] M. Medley, *Metalwork and Chinese ceramics*, pp. 17–18.

[3] C. Locsin, *A group of painted wares from Chi-chou*, Manila Trade Pottery Seminar, No. 6, 1968, p. 2.

it seems more likely that the common elements derive from the overall artistic climate of Kiangsi during a period when relationships were close and easily maintained through commercial channels. It is probable that pattern books were made up from drawings that could be fairly freely circulated. It is indeed likely that this occurred and that patterns even circulated beyond the confines of China, a point to which attention was drawn some years ago by Basil Gray[1] and which has received additional support recently from other sources.

Among the more simply painted pieces are small vases of elongated pear-shape which at present can only be found illustrated in the Chi-chou report.[2] These are much less pretentious and evidently belong to a more popular local tradition fairly low on the economic scale. Into a similar category fall also the stem-cups, one of which in the David Foundation has four-character inscriptions on each facet of the bowl, and another in the Malcolm Collection which is ornamented with highly abstract birds in flight (Plate 116A). Both these two have the strongly angular contour that is a feature already seen in some examples in the Lung-ch'üan celadons of the resist glazed series. In the Chi-chou examples, however, the bowl of the cup is thrown rather thickly and the facets on the outside are cut by hand instead of being entirely moulded as in the Lung-ch'üan series. Also unlike the celadon type the tall stem is tubular and horizontally ribbed, neither slip nor glaze reaching the foot, and the inside of the stem is left unglazed showing the rather brownish body. A peculiar feature of these stem-cups, to which Ayers first drew attention, is that there remain on the foot-ring small protuberances or 'pins' of clay on which the objects were fired and which have not always been detached, which results in some instability.[3] Whether these two stem-cups are in fact wasters is impossible to guess, but the instability is certainly rather suggestive, as some other stem-cups of the same general type but lacking the facets are quite firm, although showing traces where the 'pins' have been.

Another group of painted wares of rather a different kind should not be passed over. It consists of a number of conical bowls, a few vases of various kinds and at least one ewer. All are dark brown glazed and painted in a pale yellowish slip with a series of heart-shaped motifs filled with a knobbed scroll design. The small stout jar in the Tokyo National Museum and the bowl in Bristol City Art Gallery are excellent examples of the type (Plates 117A, B). More spontaneously

---

[1] B. Gray, 'Some Chinese drawings and their origin', *Forschungen zur Kunst Oriens*, Istanbul, 1969, pp. 159–71.

[2] *Chi-chou Yao*, Plate 47.

[3] J. Ayers, op. cit., p. 90.

painted are bowls with birds flying round a central floral element, while others, Plates 118A, B, more cursive in style almost to the point of crudeness, are similar shaped bowls with the popular prunus and crescent moon design, the execution varying greatly from one specimen to another. The outside of the bowls is usually double-glazed in a tortoise-shell effect achieved by splashing a yellowish glaze on top of the brown, as noted in Plate 110c. It is possible that all the double-glazed conical bowls with tortoiseshell effect date from the thirteenth and fourteenth centuries. All have similar bodies and rather carelessly cut foot-ring and base. In the preliminary excavations at Chi-chou some very rough pear-shaped vases in the same technique came to light, and as these are almost identical with the painted ones they would seem to be of the same approximate date.

While this last group appears in many cases to demonstrate both crudeness and carelessness, there is nothing of either to be found in the moulded white wares consisting mainly of conical and rounded bowls, most of them up to 13 or 15 cm. in diameter, some with foot-ring and some without. They are usually fired on the mouth rim, the glaze covering the whole base and foot-ring in the same way as the Ting and some of the ch'ing-pai. The moulded decoration is generally of sparingly distributed floral sprays placed about half-way up the inner wall (Plate 116B), but the design with phoenixes has also been found at the kiln sites. The white type can be divided into two classes, one, porcellanous in body, just off-white and rather dry in texture with a slightly cream toned glaze colour in the final state, and the other much finer class, which is true porcelain, generally smaller in size and decorated with the familiar prunus and crescent moon (Plate 119A). These are more thickly constructed, as one would perhaps expect with the relatively non-plastic pure porcelain, and the glaze too is thicker and rather more glossy. This is a superior ware over which considerable care has been taken, and the glaze reaches so close to the rim that at first sight it seems to run right over it, but in fact a fine unglazed edge is a regular feature. The moulded decoration may also occur on a similar porcelain body covered with a pale celadon type glaze (Plate 119B). These wares can be easily distinguished from the Lung-ch'üan wares by the pure whiteness of body. The same design can be found incised and carved in both the white and the celadon type of the same high quality.

One final type of white ware belonging to a group of southern wares often known by the name ch'ing-pai, which has been attributed to Chi-chou, but which has not yet been published as having come from that site, is a group of vases of exceptionally light weight with an almost chalky body, ill-fitting transparent yellowish or light bluish toned glaze. Most pieces are constructed from a series of moulded parts carelessly luted together one on top of another. Confined to the body the moulded decoration is somewhat naturally ordered in bands. The motifs include phoenix, dragons, flowers and diapers of various kinds and occasionally petals radiating up or downwards round the swell of the body. The glaze is of poor quality, decaying very easily in most cases and often peeling off over the decoration and joins in the body as well as along any sharp edge. While most pieces are ostensibly white, or neutral glazed, there are a few with brown glaze, one example of which is in the Hoyt Collection.[1] These are equally poor in quality and one wonders whether they were simply made for disposal with the dead; the faults are so glaringly obvious as to preclude normal practical use.

The prolific and varied output of the Chi-chou kilns is extremely impressive as is also the ingenuity of the potters in evolving decorative techniques. One type of stoneware of peculiar style which it has been suggested might have come from Chi-chou is the rather ugly so-called *guri* carved type found in recent years in the Philippines (Plate 120). This quite novel class is evidently based on carved lacquer with its bands of *ju-i* elements and spiral scrolls, to which are added angular meanders and key-frets. There is, however, no evidence either materially or stylistically to link it with Chi-chou, rather the reverse. In material and form the only affinities there are between these and the products of other kilns in the south are rather with those of Nan-chang farther north, where small brownish stoneware jars of baggy form with studs of glaze on the shoulder or round the base of the neck have been found. The same form also occurs in the *guri* type and in both cases the pieces are distinguished by the absence of a foot-ring. The nearest approximation to the shape in Chi-chou occurs in the painted type, with the spots reserved in white against a brown ground; but these are well constructed and have a clearly defined foot-ring. The vase forms in the *guri* type are also different from those of Chi-chou in having a wide body in proportion to the height and a fuller rounder curve, while the mouth rim is deliberately flattened, unlike the Chi-chou type which is only rolled or slightly thickened. In decoration, too, the divergence is marked. The *ju-i* carved motif finds no parallel at Chi-chou, nor does the so-called classic scroll motif which is found on a large scale on these extraordinary vessels. Not only are the motifs different but the conception and use of surface in design in the *guri* type is a total contradiction of that found at Chi-chou. In the yellowish

[1] *The Hoyt Collection*, Vol. 1, Plate 109, No. 155 in the small catalogue. Acc. No. 50.1871. It is unfortunate that the original misattribution should have been allowed to stand.

H. *Northern black-ware jar with painting in brown. Ht. 43 cm.*
Private Collection, Japan

painted wares of Chi-chou, especially on the vertical forms, the design is calculated in terms of verticality using a series of heart-shaped elements set in alternation and one above the other. The organization on the *guri* type is conceived in terms of the horizontal, a series of different motifs being ordered in bands. It is thus possible that as there is no connexion with Chi-chou a relationship should rather be sought farther north and perhaps east nearer to the lacquer manufacturing areas of Chekiang, but still perhaps in Kiangsi with Nan-chang, or even Nan-fêng as possible candidates. No evidence on the provenance of this distinctive type has yet come from China and more information is clearly needed.

TÊ-HUA WARES

The porcelain of Tê-hua, which became famous in the sixteenth and seventeenth centuries as what in Europe is termed *blanc de chine*, first began to appear as early as some time in the latter part of the Sung dynasty, but little is known of the production of these early years, or indeed of any of it until late in the Ming dynasty. It was Ch'ên Wan-li who first began investigations and his preliminary survey of the area led him to the conclusion that the early output was almost exclusively intended for export, as few pieces of the types actually found at the sites have been identified elsewhere in China.[1] So far it is only possible to indicate certain general features of form and decoration.

The pieces which we can assign with most assurance to the thirteenth and fourteenth centuries on the basis of Dr. Ch'ên's report are those that have been found in excavations in the Philippines and from undocumented sites in Indonesia. Most of these are simple bowls and boxes made using moulding techniques. The best and most easily recognized type of bowl is that taken directly from the mould with the foot left unfinished, so that instead of the conventional neatly cut foot-ring there is no more than a slight ridge with a rounded contour. The glaze, which is transparent and virtually colourless, does not reach the foot and the base is also unglazed; in many cases the mouth rim is also bare of glaze. The body is generally a very pure white and of fine grain, but in less good quality pieces the paste may be coarse and have a faint yellowish tinge, which is also imparted to the glaze, especially where this pools. On the best quality wares the pooling of the glaze usually tends to a faint blue, not unlike *ch'ing-pai* but yet distinct from it. The bowls of the best quality are remarkably trans-

[1] Ch'ên Wan-li, 'Tiao-ch'a Min-nan ku-tai yao-chih hsiao-chi', *Wên-wu*, 1957, No. 9, p. 57 et seq.

133

lucent when the glaze covers both inner and outer surfaces; the absence of glaze on any area on one of the two faces seems to inhibit translucency. On the less fine quality wares with the coarse body such translucency is not common, partly on account of the character of the paste and glaze, but also perhaps on account of a lower firing temperature, which has been too low to allow sintering of the body.

Decoration where this occurs is moulded, some bowls on the outside with a simple band of overlapping lotus petals, and some, less commonly perhaps, with floral elements freely disposed round the inside (Plate 121B). Both types have been found in the Philippines and the first type has recently been found in quite large numbers in Indonesia.

In the boxes similar characteristics of body and glaze are to be seen as in the bowls, the high-quality body fired to the correct temperature resulting in an object of unequalled character. The poorer quality boxes, which vary widely in size, are rather chalky, dry and friable, exceptionally light in weight and extremely brittle, the glaze showing a marked tendency to craze and in some cases to peel off. In shape the boxes are round with a curving lower half and a low-domed cover, both parts being pressed out in moulds in which the decoration is incorporated (Plate 121A). There is no foot-ring, the base being perfectly flat, or slightly concave due to sagging in the kiln, since the base section seems to have been fired on the rim despite the fact that the glaze rarely reached the base. The decorations most commonly used are based on scrolling motifs of various kinds strongly reminiscent of *guri* type lacquer, or based on varieties of simple floral scrolls and sprays. Those with flower sprays in a central panel on the top are less common than the rest, and those known are generally of rather good quality. The smaller sized boxes ranging from about 8 cm. in diameter up to 13 or 15 cm. are particularly common among the Philippine material, but a number of very fine large ones have also come to light over the last ten years.

BIBLIOGRAPHY

Addis, J. M., 'A group of underglaze red', *Transactions of the Oriental Ceramic Society*, **31**, 1957–59, pp. 15–38.

—, 'A group of underglaze red: a postscript', *Transactions of the Oriental Ceramic Society*, **36**, 1964–66, pp. 89–102.

Ayers, J., 'Some characteristic wares of the Yüan dynasty', *Transactions of the Oriental Ceramic Society*, **29**, 1954–55, pp. 69–90.

—, *Chinese and Korean Pottery and Porcelain (The Seligman Collection of Oriental Art*, Vol. 2), London, 1964.

—, *The Baur Collection: Chinese Ceramics*, Geneva, 1968.

Billington, D. M., *The Technique of Pottery*, London, 1962.

Bushell, S. W., *Oriental Ceramic Art*, New York, 1899.

—, *Description of Chinese Pottery and Porcelain, being a translation of the T'ao Shuo*, Oxford, 1910.

Garner, Sir Harry, *Oriental Blue and White*, London, 1954; 3rd edn., 1970.

Gompertz, G. St. G. M., *Chinese Celadon Wares*, London, 1958.

Green, D., *Understanding Pottery Glazes*, London, 1963.

Hobson, R. L., 'Blue and White before the Ming', *Old Furniture*, **VI**, 1929, pp. 3–8.

—, *The Catalogue of the George Eumorfopoulos Collection of Chinese, Korean and Persian Pottery and Porcelain*, London, 1925–28.

Lane, A., *Early Islamic Pottery*, London, 1947.

—, *Later Islamic Pottery*, London, 1957.

—, 'The Gagnières-Fonthill vase: a Chinese porcelain of about 1300', *Burlington Magazine*, CIII, 1961, pp. 124–32.

Lee, J. G., 'Some pre-Ming blue and white', *Archives of the Chinese Art Society of America*, **6**, 1952, pp. 33–40.

Lee, S. E., *Chinese Art under the Mongols: the Yüan Dynasty, 1279–1368*, Cleveland, 1968.

Locsin, L. and C., *Oriental Ceramics discovered in the Philippines*, Tokyo and Rutland, Vermont, 1968.

Medley, M., *Metalwork and Chinese ceramics* (Percival David Foundation Monograph Series, No. 2), London, 1972.

BIBLIOGRAPHY

Oriental Ceramic Society, *Chinese Translation Series*, from No. 1, 1967.

Osaka: Fujita Bijutsu-kan, *Fujita bijutsu-kan shōzōin zuroku* (Illustrated catalogue. Masterpieces in the Fujita Museum of Art), Osaka, 1954.

Pope, J. A., *Chinese Porcelains from the Ardebil Shrine*, Washington, 1956.

—, *Fourteenth Century Blue and White: a group of Chinese porcelains in the Topkapu Sarayi Müzesi, Istanbul* (Freer Gallery of Art, Occasional Papers, II, 1), Washington, 1952.

—, 'An annotated bibliography of Ming blue and white', *Far Eastern Ceramic Bulletin*, 10, 1950, pp. 72–89.

—, 'Two Chinese porcelains from the Umezawa Collection', *Far Eastern Ceramic Bulletin*, 41, 1959, pp. 15–22.

Sekai Tōji Zenshū ('Catalogue of World Ceramics'), X–XI, Tokyo, 1955.

Shira, S. and W. E. Cox, 'The earliest blue and white wares of China', *Far Eastern Ceramic Bulletin*, 7, 1949, pp. 12–17, 40–50.

Sickman, L., 'A ch'ing-pai porcelain figure bearing a date', *Archives of the Chinese Art Society of America*, 15, 1961, p. 34.

Sullivan, M., *Chinese Ceramics, Bronzes and Jades in the Collection of Sir Alan and Lady Barlow*, London, 1963.

Tokyo National Museum, *Illustrated Catalogues of the Tokyo National Museum: Chinese Ceramics*, Tokyo, 1965.

Wirgin, Jan, 'Some ceramic wares from Chi-chou', *Bulletin of the Museum of Far Eastern Antiquities*, 34, 1962, pp. 53–71.

—, *Sung Ceramic Designs*, Stockholm, 1970.

Zimmermann, Ernst, *Altchinesische Porzellane im Alten Serai* (*Meisterwerke der türkische Museen zu Konstantinopel*, Band 2), Berlin and Leipzig, 1930.

Ch'iang Hsüan-tai, *Chi-chou yao* ('Chi-chou wares'), Peking, 1958.

Chin Tsu-ming, *Lung-ch'üan Chi-k'ou ch'ing-tz'ǔ chih tiao-ch'a chilüeh* ('Short report on the celadon kilns at Chi-k'ou near Lung-ch'üan), *K'ao-ku*, 1962, 10, pp. 535–8.

Chu Po-ch'ien, *Chê-chiang shêng Lung-ch'üan ch'ing-tz'ǔ chih tiao-ch'a fa-chü tê chu-yao shou-huo* ('Report on the excavation of celadon kiln sites in Lung-ch'uan in Chekiang Province'), *Wên-wu*, 1963, 1, pp. 27–35.

Fu-liang Hsien Chih ('Gazetteer and History of Fu-liang Hsien'), K'ang-hsi edn., 1683.

INDEX

INDEX

INDEX

1A. *Bowl with incised design. Diam. 17·6 cm. Barlow Collection*

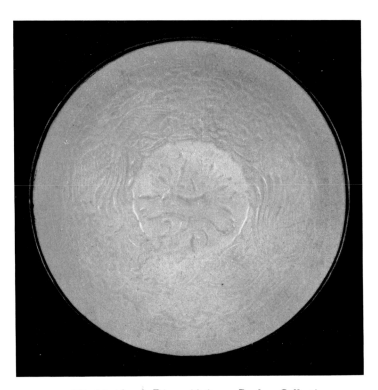

1B. *Moulded bowl. Diam. 18·8 cm. Barlow Collection*

2A. *Moulded box. Diam. 5·6 cm. Capt. Dugald Malcolm*

2B. *Moulded bowl. Diam. 19·4 cm. Ashmolean Museum*

3. *Vase with incised design. Ht.* 28·5 *cm. Royal Ontario Museum*

4. Mei-p'ing *with carved design. Ht.* 33·4 *cm. St. Louis Museum of Art*

5. Mei-p'ing *with incised design. Ht.* 31·9 *cm. Museum of Fine Arts, Boston*

6B. *Vase with slip relief. Ht. 28·1 cm.*
Ashmolean Museum

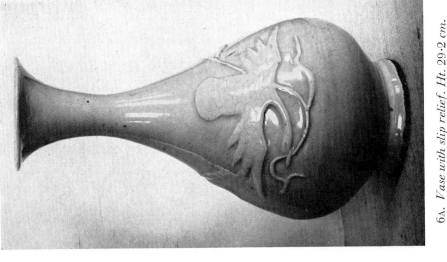

6A. *Vase with slip relief. Ht. 29·2 cm.*
Cincinnati Museum of Art

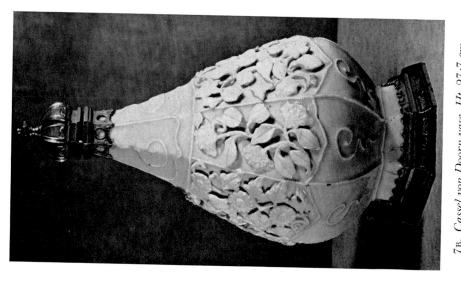

7B. *Cassel von Doorn vase. Ht. 27·7 cm.*
Victoria and Albert Museum

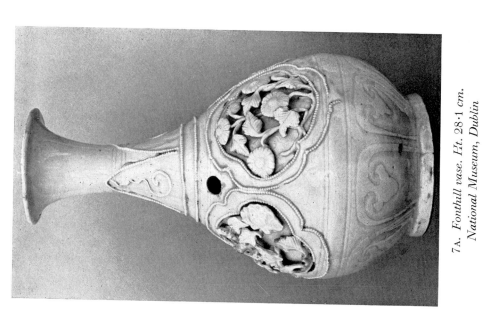

7A. *Fonthill vase. Ht. 28·1 cm.*
National Museum, Dublin

8A. *Stem cup with reliefs. Ht. 9·2 cm. City Art Gallery, Bristol*

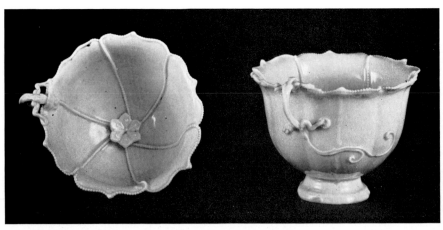

8B. *Cup with reliefs. Ht. 6·4 cm. The Cleveland Museum of Art*

9. *Vase and stand with reliefs. Ht. 23·9 cm. Brundage Collection*

10. *Ewer with reliefs. Ht.* 34·3 *cm. The Art Institute, Chicago*

11. *Figure of lion. Ht. 23·1 cm. Ashmolean Museum*

12. *Figure of Kuan Yin. Ht.* 51·4 *cm. W. R. Nelson Gallery, Kansas City*

13. *Figure of Manjusri. Ht. 50·8 cm. Metropolitan Museum*

14A, B. *T'ien-shun dish, 1328 A.D. Diam. 20·9 cm.*
Percival David Foundation

15A, B. *Dragon dish, moulded. Diam. 17·8 cm.*
Victoria and Albert Museum

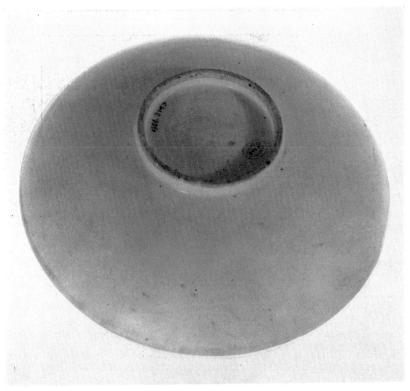

16A, B. *Moulded chrysanthemum dish. Diam.* 20·1 *cm. Ashmolean Museum*

17. *Moulded dish from Pao-ting hoard. Diam.* 16·2 *cm. Hopei Museum*

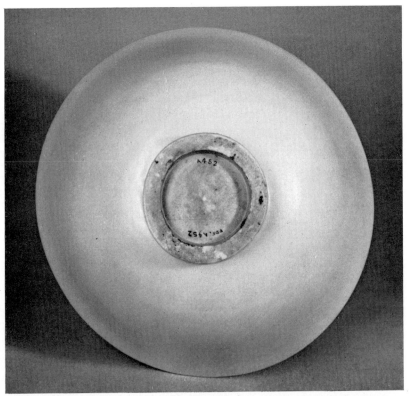

18A, B. *Moulded* Shu-fu *bowl. Diam.* 20·8 *cm. Percival David Foundation*

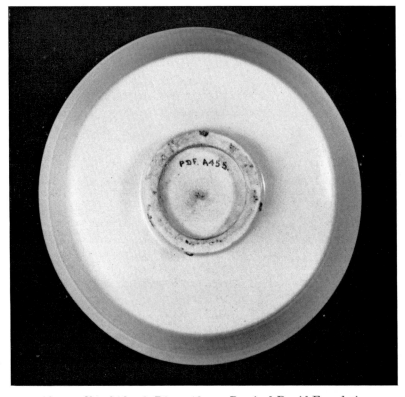

19A, B. Shu-fu *bowl*. *Diam*. 12 *cm*. *Percival David Foundation*

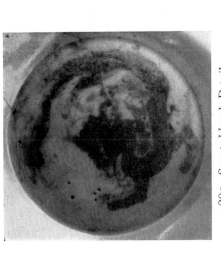

20c. *Spouted bowl. Detail*

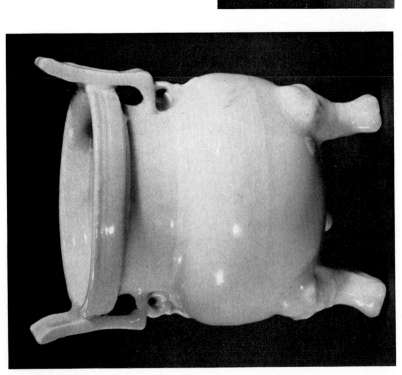

20b. *Spouted bowl. Diam. 16·5 cm. Capt. Dugald Malcolm*

20a. *Tripod vase. Ht. 14·9 cm. Mr. and Mrs. Eugene Bernat*

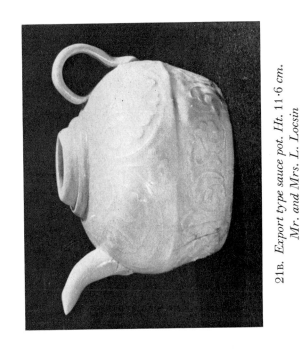

21B. *Export type sauce pot. Ht. 11·6 cm.*
Mr. and Mrs. L. Locsin

21A. *Export type sauce pot. Ht. 8·2 cm.*
Mr. and Mrs. L. Locsin

22. *Lobed plate. Diam. 17·6 cm. Percival David Foundation*

23. *Copper-red painted vase. Ht. 30·5 cm.*
Percival David Foundation

24. *David Temple vase. Ht. 63·6 cm.*
Percival David Foundation

25. *Vase with dragon. Ht. 24·8 cm. Mrs. Alfred Clark*

26A. *Plate. Diam. 45·7 cm. Formerly Sotheby's*

26B. *Plate. Diam. 45·1 cm. Topkapu Seray*

27. *Plate. Diam.* 44·5 *cm. Los Angeles County Museum*

28A. *Plate. Diam. 45·9 cm. Ardebil*

28B. *Plate. Diam. 39·9 cm. Ardebil*

29A. *Plate. Diam. 45·7 cm. Ardebil*

29B. *Plate. Diam. 45·4 cm. Topkapu Seray*

30. *Plate. Diam. 41 cm. Topkapu Seray*

31. Plate. Diam. 41 cm. British Museum

32A. *Plate. Diam. 47 cm. British Museum*

32B. *Plate. Diam. 47 cm. Ardebil*

33A. *Plate. Diam.* 46·4 *cm. Topkapu Seray*

33B. *Plate. Diam.* 45·4 *cm. Topkapu Seray*

34A. *Plate. Diam.* 45·7 *cm. Victoria and Albert Museum*

34B. *Plate. Diam.* 40 *cm. Formerly Sotheby's*

35A. *Plate. Diam. 39·4 cm. Yale Peabody Museum*

35B. *Plate. Diam. 46·4 cm. The Art Institute of Chicago*

36A. *Plate. Diam. 46·4 cm. Palace Museum, Taiwan*

36B. *Plate. Diam. 46·8 cm. Palace Museum, Taiwan*

37. *Plate. Diam.* 55·1 *cm. Palace Museum, Taiwan*

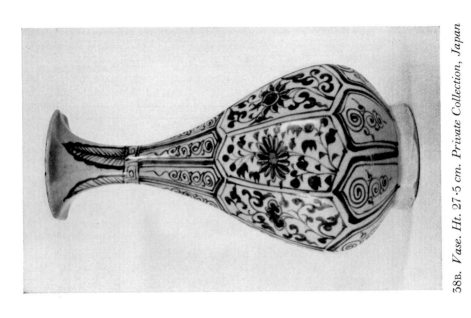

38B. *Vase. Ht. 27·5 cm. Private Collection, Japan*

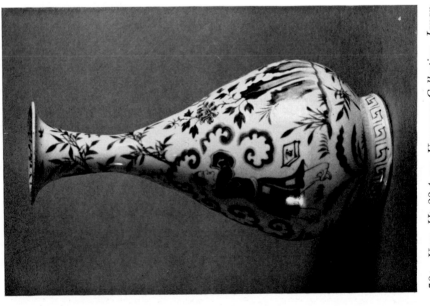

38A. *Vase. Ht. 28·1 cm. Umezawa Collection, Japan*

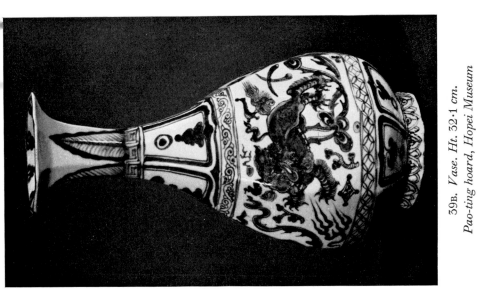

39B. *Vase. Ht. 32·1 cm.*
Pao-ting hoard, Hopei Museum

39A. *Ewer. Ht. 23·5 cm.*
Pao-ting hoard, Hopei Museum

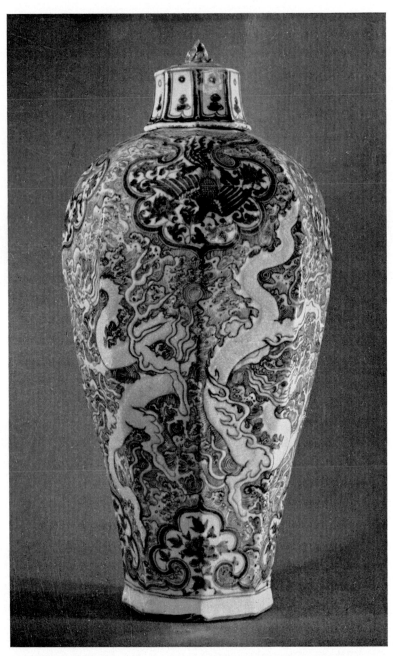

40. Mei-p'ing. *Ht. 51·4 cm. Pao-ting hoard, Hopei Museum*

41. *Gourd vase. Ht. 58·2 cm. Private Collection, Japan*

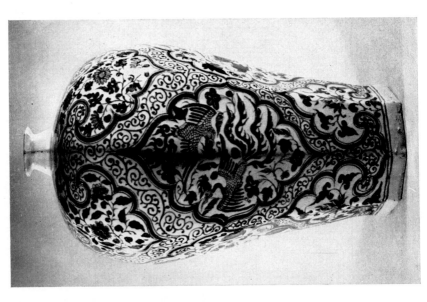

42B. *Vase. Ht. 45 cm. Fitzwilliam Museum*

42A. Mei-p'ing. Ht. 44·5 cm.

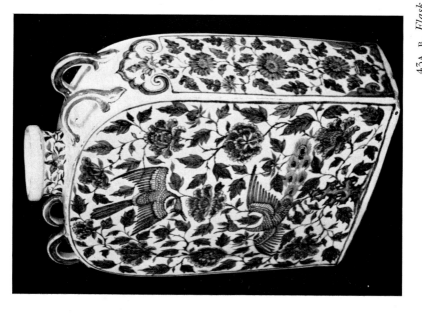

43A, B. *Flask. Ht. 36·5 cm. Ardebil*

44B. *Flask. Ht. 57·9 cm. Sir Harry and Lady Garner*

44A. *Wine jar. Ht. 30·5 cm. British Museum*

45B. *Wine jar. Ht. 39·4 cm. Cleveland Museum of Art*

45A. *Wine jar. Ht. 37 cm. Museum of Fine Arts, Boston*

46. Mei-p'ing. *Ht.* 41·9 *cm. Sir Harry and Lady Garner*

47A, B. *Bowl. Diam. 34 cm. Topkapu Seray*

48. Gourd vase. Ht. 59·9 cm. Topkapu Seray

49. Mei-p'ing. *Ht.* 38 *cm. Formerly Christie's*

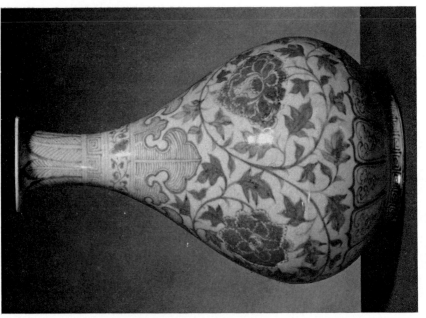

50A. Copper-red vase. Ht. 33 cm. Lord Trevelyan

50B. Copper-red ewer. Ht. 33 cm. Brooklyn Museum of Art

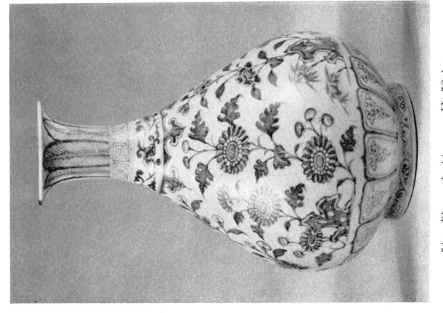

51A. *Copper-red vase. Ht. 31·1 cm. Sir Lionel Lamb*

51B. *Blue and white vase. Ht. 32·1 cm.*
Philadelphia Museum of Art

52A. *Copper-red bowl. Diam. 23·4 cm. Hosokawa Collection*

52B. *Blue and white plate. Diam. 46·4 cm. Palace Museum, Taiwan*

53. *Copper-red jar. Ht. 50·8 cm. Private Collection, Japan*

54. *Copper-red* mei-p'ing. *Ht.* 36·4 *cm. Nanking Museum*

55A. *Blue and white plate. Diam.* 19·7 *cm. Sir John Addis*

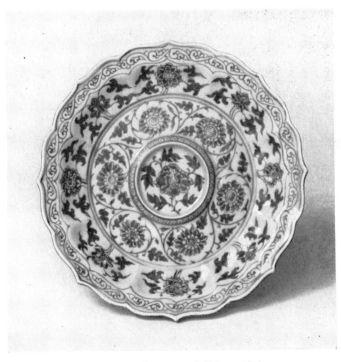

55B. *Copper-red cup-stand. Diam.* 19·1 *cm.*
Avery Brundage Collection

56A. *Copper-red* kendi. *Ht. 15·2 cm. Miss Ruth Dreyfus*

56B. *Blue spouted bowl, gilt. Diam. 13·1 cm.*
Pao-ting hoard, Hopei Museum

57A, B. *White on blue spouted bowl. Diam. 13·3 cm.*
Victoria and Albert Museum

58. *Vase, dated 1327. Ht. 71·1 cm. Percival David Foundation*

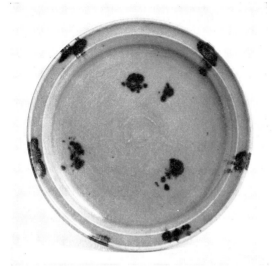

59A. Tobi-seiji *plate. Diam.* 16·5 *cm.*
Avery Brundage Collection

59B. Tobi-seiji *vase. Ht.* 27·3 *cm.*
Percival David Foundation

60A. *Bowl with impressed mark. Diam. 15·9 cm. Percival David Foundation*

60B. *Bowl with inverted rim. Diam. 21·4 cm. Percival David Foundation*

61A. *Bowl with impressed flower. Diam.* 15·9 *cm.*
Percival David Foundation

61B. *Bowl with fish in relief. Diam.* 15·2 *cm. Percival David Foundation*

62B. *Plate with dragon reliefs. Diam. 16·3 cm.*
Formerly G. de Menasce Collection

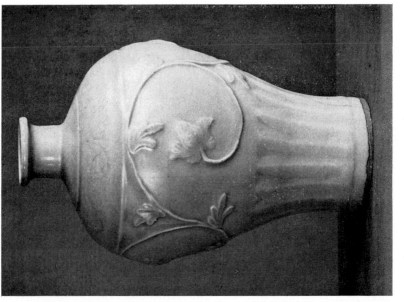

62A. Mei-p'ing with reliefs. Ht. 22·3 cm.
Seligman Collection

63. *Rectangular flask with relief. Ht. 31·5 cm. Percival David Foundation*

64A. *Plate with fruit sprays. Diam.* 16·3 *cm.*
Formerly G. de Menasce Collection

64B. *Plate with peach sprays and birds. Diam.* 16·5 *cm.*
Percival David Foundation

65. *Prunus plate. Diam.* 16·5 *cm. British Museum*

66. *Vase with reserved panels. Ht.* 24·8 *cm. Percival David Foundation*

67A, B. *Stem cup with reserved panels. Ht.* 13·3 *cm.*
Formerly G. de Menasce Collection

68A. *Square dish, moulded. Ht. 9 cm.*
Formerly G. de Menasce Collection

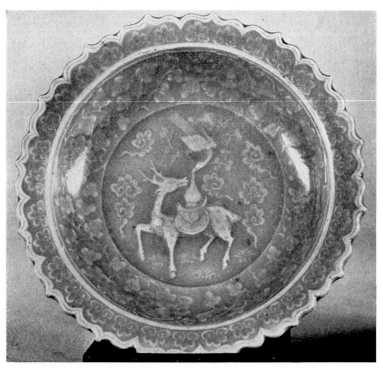

68B. *Moulded plate. Diam. 15·2 cm. Avery Brundage Collection*

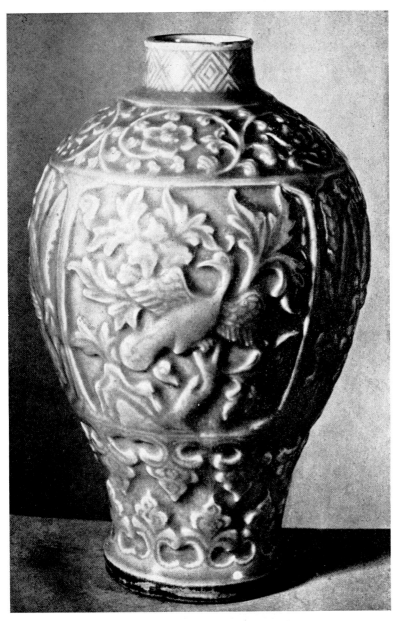

69. *Moulded* mei-p'ing. *Ht. 35·3 cm. Formerly Russell Collection*

70A. *Carved jar and cover. Ht. 22·9 cm. Philadelphia Museum of Art*

70B, C. *Details of base and interior*

71. *Carved plate. Diam.* 35·6 *cm. Mr. and Mrs. L. Locsin*

72A, B. *Carved bowl. Diam.* 41·9 *cm. Percival David Foundation*

73. *Carved plate with reliefs. Diam. 41 cm. Topkapu Seray*

74. *Carved fluted plate. Diam. 44·5 cm. Topkapu Seray*

75. *Carved vase with vines. Ht.* 30·5 *cm.*
Formerly G. de Menasce Collection

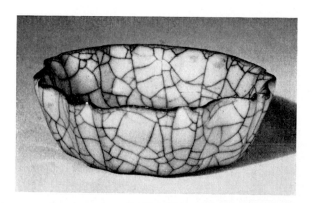

76A. *Kuan type brush washer. Diam. 9·5 cm. Percival David Foundation*

76B. *Kuan type moulded* kuei. *Diam. 27·3 cm. Percival David Foundation*

77. *Lung-ch'üan tsun. Ht.* 20·3 *cm.*
Percival David Foundation

78A. *Moulded bowl. Diam.* 12·1 *cm. Ashmolean Museum*

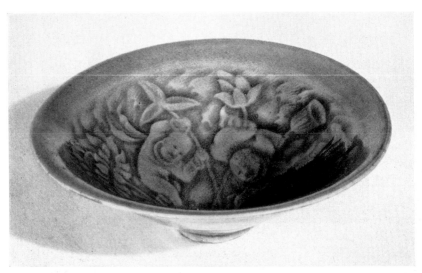

78B. *Moulded bowl. Diam.* 15·5 *cm. Barlow Collection*

79A. *Carved bowl. Diam.* 21·6 *cm. Barlow Collection*

79B. *Carved* Hsiu-nu *bowl. Diam.* 21·4 *cm. Barlow Collection*

80A. *Moulded dish. Diam. 16·3 cm.*
Formerly Eumorfopoulos Collection

80B. *Moulded dish. Diam. 10·7 cm.*
Victoria and Albert Museum

81A. *Tripod. Ht.* 10·4 *cm. Percival David Foundation*

81B. *Two bowls. Diam.* 12 *cm. Baur Foundation*

82. *Green Chün tripod. Ht.* 29·9 *cm. Philadelphia Museum of Art*

83A. *Splashed jar. Ht. 12·4 cm. Victoria and Albert Museum*

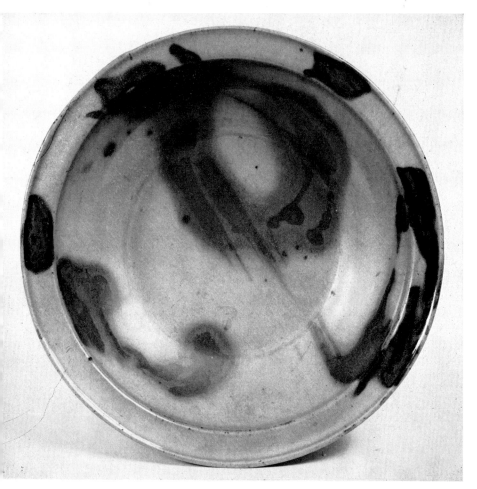

83B. *Splashed basin. Diam. 32 cm. Mount Trust*

84A. *Spouted bowl. Diam.* 17·2 *cm. Baur Foundation*

84B. *Pillow. W.* 31·8 *cm. Metropolitan Museum, New York*

85A. *Numbered narcissus bowl. Diam. 21·1 cm. Percival David Foundation*

85B. *Numbered flower pot. Diam. 24·8 cm. Percival David Foundation*

86A, B. *Carved dish. Diam.* 16·8 *cm. Percival David Foundation*

87A. *Incised plate. Diam. 21 cm. Percival David Foundation*

87B. *Incised plate. Diam. 23·9 cm. British Museum*

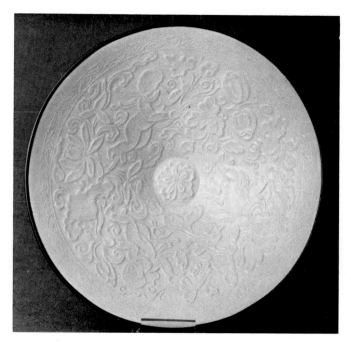

88A. *Moulded bowl. Diam.* 21·5 *cm. British Museum*

88B. *Moulded bowl. Diam.* 15·5 *cm.*
Victoria and Albert Museum

89A. *Moulded plate. Diam.* 19·2 *cm. British Museum*

89B. *Moulded plate. Diam.* 21·5 *cm.*
Percival David Foundation

90A. *Moulded plate. Diam.* 22·2 *cm. Percival David Foundation*

90B. *Moulded bowl. Diam.* 19·8 *cm. Mrs. Alfred Clark*

91A. *Moulded dish. Diam. 10·7 cm. Victoria and Albert Museum*

91B. *Moulded bowl. Diam. 23·5 cm. Percival David Foundation*

92. *Incised plate. Diam.* 25·6 *cm. British Museum*

93. *Painted vase. Ht.* 24·1 *cm. Seattle Art Museum*

94A. *Painted bowl. Diam. 11·4 cm. Private Collection, Japan*

94B. *Painted vase. Ht. 23·5 cm. Seligman Collection*

95A. *Painted dish. Diam. 17·8 cm. Seligman Collection*

95B. *Painted jar. Ht. 36·2 cm. Peking Palace Museum*

96A. *Fragment of painted jar. Ht. 30·5 cm. Pa-ts'un find*

96B. *Painted wine jar. Ht. 31·8 cm. Avery Brundage Collection*

97. *Painted vase. Ht. 88·9 cm. Seattle Art Museum*

98. *Painted storage jar. Ht. 91·5 cm. Art Institute, Chicago*

99A. *Landscape painted pillow. L. 43·3 cm. Victoria and Albert Museum*

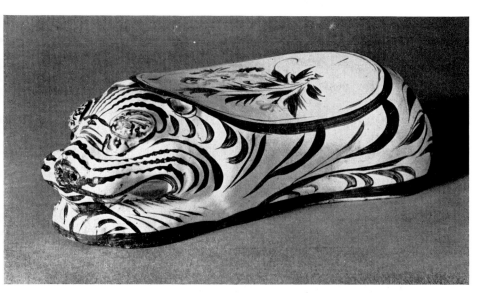

99B. *Tiger headrest. L. 36·8 cm. Victoria and Albert Museum*

100B. *Painted jar. Ht. 38·1 cm. Avery Brundage Collection*

100A. *Painted jar. Ht. 25·5 cm. British Museum*

C.

101A. *Polychrome dated bowl. Diam. 15·5 cm.*
Tokyo National Museum
101B. *Polychrome bowl. Diam. 17·1 cm. Baur Foundation*
101C. *Polychrome bowl. Diam. 23·5 cm.*
Detroit Institute of Art

A.

B.

102B. *Polychrome figure. Ht. 24·1 cm.*
Metropolitan Museum

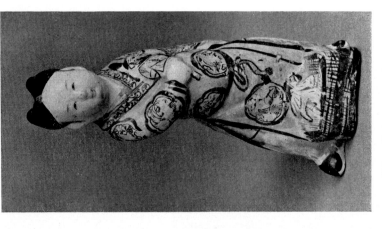

102A. *Polychrome figure.*
Ht. 17·1 cm. Baur Foundation

103B. *Polychrome jar. Ht. 31·8 cm. Metropolitan Museum*

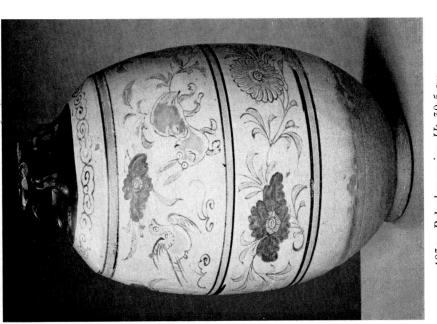

103A. *Polychrome jar. Ht. 30·5 cm.*
Victoria and Albert Museum

104B. *Sgraffiato basin. Diam.* 35·6 *cm. Tokyo National Museum*

104A. *Sgraffiato bowl. Diam.* 27·9 *cm. Mount Trust*

105B. *Carved jar. Ht. 38·4 cm. Formerly Eumorfopoulos Collection*

105A. *Carved vase. Ht. 33 cm.*
Private Collection, Japan

106A. *Cut-glaze jar. Ht. 24·4 cm. Victoria and Albert Museum*

106B. *Cut-glaze jar. Ht. 33 cm. Tokyo National Museum*

107. *Cut-glaze vase. Ht. 27·9 cm. St. Louis Museum of Art*

108B. *Cut-glaze vase. Ht. 29 cm. Baur Foundation*

108A. *Shansi type cut-glaze bowl. Ht. 23·5 cm.*
Tokyo National Museum

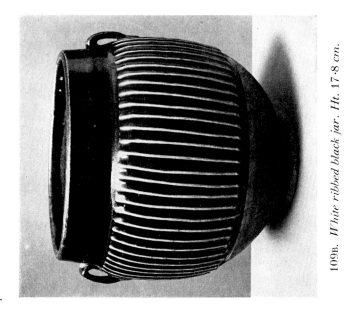

109B.   *White ribbed black jar. Ht. 17·8 cm.*
Victoria and Albert Museum

109A.   *Brown painted vase. Ht. 27·4 cm.*
British Museum

110A. *Leaf* temmoku *bowl. Diam. 15 cm. Baur Foundation*

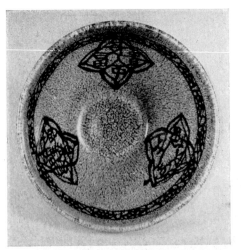 

110B, C. *Paper-cut bowl. Diam. 12·2 cm. Tokyo National Museum*

111A. *Cut-glaze vase. Ht. 13·7 cm. City Art Gallery, Bristol*

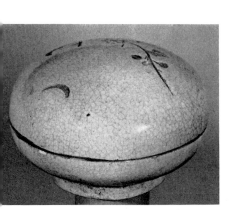

111B, C. *Incised box. Diam. 8·1 cm. Mr. and Mrs. Eugene Bernat*

112B. *Resist vase. Ht. 26·2 cm.*
St. Louis Museum of Art

112A. *Resist vase. Ht. 19 cm.*
Barlow Collection

113B. *Painted jar. Diam. 12·7 cm. Mrs. B. Virata*

113A. *Painted jar. Diam. 8·9 cm.*
Mr. and Mrs. L. Locsin

114. *Painted vase. Ht. 44·8 cm. British Museum*

115. *Painted vase. Ht. 26 cm. Mrs. Lehmann*

116A. *Painted stem cup. Ht. 11·4 cm. Capt. Dugald Malcolm*

116B. *Moulded white saucer. Diam. 14·6 cm. Barlow Collection*

117A. *Slip-painted bowl. Diam. 12·5 cm.*
City Art Gallery, Bristol

117B. *Slip-painted jar. Ht. 23·1 cm. Tokyo National Museum*

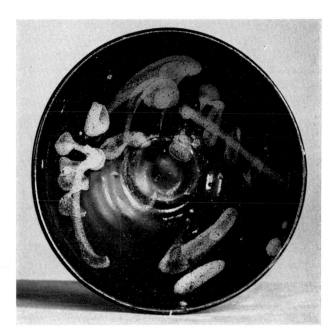

118A. *Slip-painted bowl. Diam.* 11·4 *cm.*
Victoria and Albert Museum

118B. *Slip-painted bowl. Diam.* 12·5 *cm.*
Victoria and Albert Museum

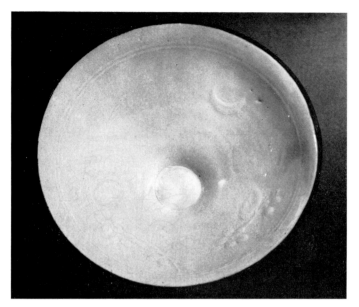

119A. *White ware bowl. Diam.* 13 *cm.*
Mr. and Mrs. Eugene Bernat

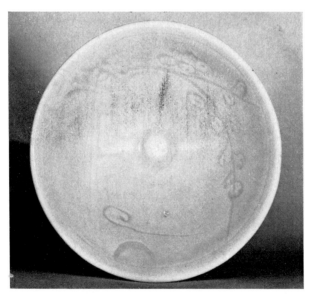

119B. *White ware bowl with celadon glaze. Diam.* 10·2 *cm.*
Mr. and Mrs. Eugene Bernat

120. *Guri ware jar and vase. Hts. 15·2 cm. Elizalde Collection*
26·7 cm. de Santos Collection

121A. Té-hua box. Diam. 14·6 cm. Mrs. J. Allison

121B. Té-hua bowl. Diam. 15·2 cm. Mr. and Mrs. L. Locsin

122A. *Early plate. Above, peony scroll reserved in white*
Below, early form of wave border

122B. *Later plate. Above, lotus scroll in blue*
Below, segmented wave border

122C. *Classic scroll*

122D. *'Knobbed' classic scroll*

123A. *Above, lotus panels*
Below, lāmalif *panels enclosing emblems*

123B. *Cloud-collar element, enclosing*
pheasant on blackberry-lily ground

123C. *Normal peony flower*

123D. *Split peony flower*

124A. *Earlier type of key-fret*

124B. *Later type of key-fret (S-Form)*

124C. *Blackberry-lily border*

124D. *Late Fourteenth century type of wave border*
Compare with early form in Plate 122A